HAPPINESS

THE

Forgotten Ingredient

Books by Kenny Felderstein

Never Buy A Hat If Your Feet Are Cold - Taking Charge Of Your Career And Your Life

The Year Of My Death

A True Leader Has Presence - The Six Building Blocks To Presence

Happiness The Forgotten Ingredient

HAPPINESS
THE *Forgotten Ingredient*

KENNY FELDERSTEIN

AUTHOR OF "NEVER BUY A HAT IF YOUR FEET ARE COLD - TAKING CHARGE OF YOUR CAREER AND YOUR LIFE"

iUniverse, Inc.
Bloomington

Happiness The Forgotten Ingredient

iUniverse books may be ordered through booksellers or by contacting:

iUniverse
1663 Liberty Drive
Bloomington, IN 47403
www.iuniverse.com
1-800-Authors (1-800-288-4677)

ISBN: 978-1-4759-8341-8 (sc)
ISBN: 978-1-4759-8342-5 (ebk)

Printed in the United States of America

iUniverse rev. date: 03/25/2013

CONTENTS

DISCLAIMER

The comments by the author, Kenny Felderstein, are his own. They represent his thoughts, feelings and opinions Kenny Felderstein is dedicated to assisting the reader of this book in taking charge of their career and their life. He is not a doctor or therapist. The information he will give the reader comes from many years of executive management in business and personal life experiences—not just from books. He has come from meager roots to achieve Vice President and President level positions in both small and very large corporations. He has changed careers and taken demotions for the sole purpose of enhancing his happiness. He has overcome divorce and family tragedy while creating a rewarding and happy life.

The information and suggestions he will give the reader is just that—information and suggestions. What the reader does with this information is up to the individual.

It's your life not his. It's within your power to make the changes that will lead to a happier career and/or a happier life. Kenny Felderstein is your facilitator *not* your decision maker.

Now is your time to take charge of your career and your life. Now it is your time to take control of *your* happiness—YOU DESERVE IT!!!!

To all the people, in every country, who have been reading my blogs. Thank you for your interest and feedback.

Jerry, thanks for your support

To my wife who always makes me feel mighty—mighty real.

FROM THE AUTHOR

KENNY FELDERSTEIN

Why Do I Blog?

After publishing my third book "A True Leader Has Presence—The Six Building Blocks To Presence," I realized writing a book is a long tedious challenge. The writing can take many, many months or even years. The worst part is the editing. Before I feel I have something that's ready to publish, I have readers read my manuscript. These readers are people who I believe are the book's target audience.

These readers give me a vast amount of feedback which leads to more months of editing. By the end of the process, the book that was a labor of love when I started became something I never wanted to read again.

For my next project, I wrote a treatment of my fourth book. It is going to be a novel about how something that starts out good for all people turns out to be bad for all people. It will be called "For The Good Of The People."

During the time I was writing the treatment I was also mentoring several people. The goal of my mentoring is to help people who are not getting all the happiness they deserve, to understand how they can make changes that will bring more happiness into their lives. I help them take control of their careers, their lives and their happiness.

While contemplating writing my fourth book, I decided to write a blog about what I teach—happiness. It was great. It took me an hour and a half to write and only fifteen minutes to edit. It was three pages instead of three hundred pages. It communicated one of the many things I already share with my clients. It was a catharsis for me to see the words on the page.

I immediately put the book on hold and started writing blogs. These blogs have had a significant effect on me. They remind me what I have lived through and what I did to get over the things that were holding me back. These blogs enable me to share my thoughts on happiness to people I would otherwise never be able to reach. I'm blown away that people in Russia, Germany,

Latvia (I don't even know where Latvia is), Ukraine, Brazil, United Kingdom, South Korea and Saudi Arabia read my blogs.

These blogs enable me to get instant feedback from many of my readers. This feedback really feels good even if they take issue with something I've said. Most of all, these blogs allow me to share with you very personal and emotional feelings I have inside me.

Putting those feelings on the written page is releasing. It's like an exercise I teach my clients.

"Put your left hand and your right hand, facing each other, to your chest bone at the center of your breasts. Take a deep breath and at the same time throw your hands to the sky while letting out your breath."

This exercise is a way of releasing stress. Take something inside you that needs releasing and do this exercise. Don't just do it once, do it multiple times until the bad stuff inside goes away. If you want, while throwing out your hands to the sky, you can scream out the words from the movie "Network":

"I'm mad as hell and I'm not going to take it anymore."

It's important for your happiness to share the most personal and emotional things stuffed inside you. If you have the guts to do so, say it to someone/anyone who is truly interested. Just saying it out loud to yourself is not good enough. Let someone/anyone hear it. Let someone/anyone read it.

Take judgment out of your mind. Why do you care if they judge you? What's it your business if they're weak minded and feel threatened by your disclosure. Putting up barriers so you won't be judged is the wrong answer. Take a deep breath and let it all hang out.

The more you reveal the happier you become.

BLOG# 1

Have You Laughed Today?

I find something to make me laugh every day. Not every minute of every day, but for sure every day. My wife and my friends think I'm strange because I watch Jerry Springer while riding on my spin bike. I know it's all made up bullshit, but it makes me laugh. When the audience starts screaming "Jerry, Jerry, Jerry" I'm raising my arms and screaming with them.

Am I stupid for watching the show—NO! Why, because laughing makes me happy. Laughing releases endorphins in your frontal lobe that controls your mood. When laughing, these endorphins release stress and create a positive attitude. Endorphin release happens when you do other things—some positive and some negative. Exercise releases endorphins, eating sweets releases endorphins, doing drugs releases endorphins, true love releases endorphins and great sex releases endorphins.

I vote for laughter, exercising, love and sex. One of the reasons some people get addicted is because they crave the endorphin rush. If I'm going to get addicted I want it to be because I'm laughing too much, exercising too much, loving too much and having too much great sex.

Not all of us have control over how much we exercise. Illness, broken bones, work and family, etc. etc. can limit the amount of exercise we get. Not all of us have control over how much we love. Growing up in a very bad situation makes some people put up so many barriers that they find it hard to love. Not all of us have control over how much sex we get. The reason is because it takes two to tango to have great sex.

Sooo, if we can't control how much exercise, love and sex we have, then why not focus on the thing we can control—laughter. There is always enough time to laugh. There are always enough things going on that can make you laugh. The issue is, do you go looking for laughter or are you hoping it will just happen? Do you view life as being so hard that there is no laughter available out there? Do you believe that laughing won't change a thing in your unhappy life?

I hope you are not one of those people. I hope you realize that laughter will give you positive energy which will lead to a happier life. I hope you seek out positive energy people that make you laugh. I hope you become a positive energy person by laughing a lot. I hope you start out each day looking for things to laugh about instead of waiting for the outside world to make you laugh.

It's easy if you don't make it hard. Remember, if all else fails, you can always watch Jerry Springer and laugh your ass off while cheering "Jerry, Jerry, Jerry."

BLOG# 2

Reach Out

My parents were two wonderful people who never would "rock the boat" when it came to conflict. My mother's Jewish saying was: "sha still"—be quiet. What she meant was, don't fight back—rollover. My father was the same.

My sister was just the opposite. She was angry a lot and she took it out on me and them. Knowing what I know now, I believe she resented my parents because they were poor and ordinary. She never felt special and wanted them to be special so she could feel better. As you know that never works and it didn't work for her.

When she would berate my parents they would not fight back. They would never put her in her place. Maybe if they did she would have been a happier person. I know my parents would have been happier. Daily life was a struggle in my family. My sister made things worse.

I was four years younger and her actions affected my happiness at home. I resented her. I hated her. She hated me back. We yelled and fought. One day when I was twelve, in a rage, she took a butter knife and threw it at me. We never spoke again after that day.

I not only hated her, I started to resent my parents because I felt I had to always be the good son. I couldn't do anything wrong. I was the one who had to make them proud. I was the one who had to make their lives happier. If I failed, they would be crushed. They had zero expectations of my sister, but had high hopes for me. I never felt I could be good enough. I never felt I could be a happy go lucky guy. I never felt I could take risks that might fail and upset them.

I knew they loved me with all their hearts, but I also knew they were living their lives through me. It made them proud when I got a job in the computer business. It made them proud when I became a manager and then an executive. It made them proud when I went to college at night. It made them proud when I got married and had kids. I was their one resource for a happy life.

At 39, I got help with all the stuff that was inside me. One of the things I had to deal with was my anger for my sister. We had not spoken for almost thirty years. I heard through my parents that she had men problems, drinking problems, social problems and was generally unhappy.

My mentor, Bob, told me I had to find a way to love her—not for her sake, but for mine. My anger was hurting *me*. He taught me that I didn't have to love my family, but if I could find a way to love the ones I hated the most, my life would get better. Bob was right then and he is still right today.

At 41, I called my sister. She was very cold on the phone. I told her she could hang up on me, but I was going to call her at least once a week. A month later, I flew from LA to Philadelphia. I hugged my father and we cried together. That was the first time I saw him cry.

I then went over to my sister's house. She reluctantly let me in and I immediately hugged her. It was awkward, but I hung on. In a few seconds, that felt like hours, we were hugging each other. It felt so good. I felt so happy. Here was this person, who I hated for thirty years, making me cry because she hugged me back. All my anger was gone and I believed all her anger was gone.

The next years were great. We talked at least once a week. During my mentoring, Bob helped me understand why people act out the way they do—that included me. With that understanding, I was able to be sympathetic and empathetic to my sister. She and I were not that dissimilar. The stuff inside us just played out in different ways. She didn't have a happy life and became an alcoholic. I wasn't having a happy life (until I got help) and became a workaholic.

She was fighting alcoholism and at 50 she got her AA ten year token. I was so proud of her. Then the shit hit the fan. They discovered she had stage 4 ovarian cancer. She felt like all of her hope was gone and her happiness was just an illusion. I asked her to reach out to me.

I was there, helping her fight for her life. I was there helping her live the best she could for today. I told her I would love and comfort her through the worst of times.

Four years later, she went into remission. We were ecstatic. She fought the hard fight and I loved myself because I was there for her. Six months later the worst happened—the cancer came back more aggressive than before.

My sister, Shirley, died four months later. I felt so sad. However, I was also so happy I had thirteen years with her. I felt happy I could be there for her especially through the worst of times. I felt good that for the first time in a long time she had happiness in her life. I felt happy I was able to encourage her to fight this horrible disease for four years when the doctors said she only had a few months to live. I felt happy we were brother and sister for the first time.

I felt happy I overcame anger for my sister and found love.

BLOG# 3

Anyone Who Has Never Made A Mistake Has Never Tried Something New

Albert Einstein

I guess Albert was more than just a brilliant scientist. He could have mentored me when I was afraid to make a mistake. He could have mentored me when I was hesitant to take a risk. He could have mentored me when I felt safe staying with the old instead of the new.

How many mistakes have you made in your life? Did you make the same mistake more than once? How do you feel when you make a mistake? Do you try to avoid making a mistake because you get frustrated if you do so? How do you feel about someone who makes a mistake and doesn't show they feel bad about it?

How many new things have you tried? Do you feel bad when you know you should have tried something new? Do you take a step back and think about something new you could be doing today? Where are you when the group decides to try something new? Do you envy people that seem to always be willing to try something new?

I've made many mistakes. I've made the same mistake twice and have two divorces to show for it. I used to do everything I could to avoid mistakes. Like my father before and his father before, I feared taking risks. I used to feel like I was not good enough when I made a mistake. I had little tolerance for mistakes by others and really got pissed off when they didn't seem to care because I believed it reflected negatively on me.

Like my father before and his father before, I didn't try new things. In our family, we ate the same food on each day of the week. Monday was hamburgers, Tuesday was boiled chicken, Wednesday was a sandwich, etc. Every Sunday was dinner out at the same restaurant. The few vacations we took were always to the same place. When presented with an opportunity to improve his small sandwich business, my father always declined.

My saving grace, when I was on my own, was the desire to get more out of life than my father. That desire got me to take a few risks and try some new things. As I started to realize I was able to recover from my mistakes, I became willing to risk making more mistakes. My willingness to risk more mistakes enabled me to try new things.

I'm still cautious and conservative (old habits are hard to break), but I don't fear making a mistake or trying something new. My wife isn't a mistake driven new experience junkie, but she has always been out there much more than I. Over our twenty seven years, she has helped me realize the happiness of new experiences.

Where are you on this scale? Too many mistakes could lead to unhappiness. Too few risks might lead to unhappiness. Too many new experiences might not make you happy and for sure, too few new experiences will never make you a happy person.

The balance has got to be about you and how you feel about yourself. Life has so many new things to offer you. However, jumping out of an airplane might not be in your make-up. Our parents tried to prevent us from making mistakes. However, not being willing to make a mistake by quitting your current unhappy job to take one more interesting, is the core of Einstein's message.

"Anyone who has never made a mistake has never tried something new." Don't be that person. Learning from your mistakes will feed your confidence and your ego.

Having new successful experiences will enhance your love of life.

Go for it! You will fix any mistake you make. You will be able to sort out which new experience is right for you and which is not. The more you can bring yourself to take a risk, the happier you will become.

If you make more right decisions than wrong decisions your life will be better. No decision is a wrong decision.

Kenny Felderstein

BLOG# 4

Bond—James Bond

The cable TV station Encore is showing old 007 movies. I was watching the 1965 movie "Thunderball." It was a kick watching the computers they were using. They were very big and had lots of lights and switches. Some of the gadgets depicted then are just now being made. I was also shocked to think this movie was made forty seven years ago. For some of you that's twenty years older than you are now. For me, I can only wish I was 47 now.

There weren't a lot of high tech stunts. No blue screen. No animation. Just good old stunt work by real people. The thing is it didn't look any more real than the Mission Impossible of today. Great job Hollywood!

Thunderball, like many movies of that day, were very sexist. In one scene, Sean Connery (The real Bond) forces himself on a beautiful woman he just met. She resists, but he grabs her and kisses her and she just melts.

In the next scene they are waking up in bed together. Why is it I don't remember that's the way it worked? Oh, I get it—I'm Kenny Felderstein not Bond—James Bond.

Today, the writer of that scene would have been scolded and forced to change it. Today, the woman would have kicked him in the ___. I can't write it because it hurts just thinking about it. Today, the woman would be grabbing him and taking him to bed—Smith—Mary Smith.

The women had names like Pussy Galore. I don't think too many famous female actors would like to be called Pussy Galore. The only female, in these movies, that acted like the females of today was Miss Moneypenny. She knew Bond the way he was and liked him just the way he was.

Thunderball had many scenes where live sharks were being killed. This was not animation. This was not a mechanical shark, a la the movie "Jaws." These were real sharks with real harpoons piercing their flesh and killing them. Can you spell ANIMAL CRUELTY? No way would those scenes happen today—even if it's a scary shark.

I also noticed there wasn't one Black or Hispanic actor in a leading, supporting or sub-supporting role. The goodies or the baddies didn't have *one*. You would think the baddies would have at least *one*.

We all think the 50's and 60's were the good old days. The fact is those days had their problems. It wasn't so great to be Black. Women were dominated by men. Not just in the bedroom, but in many aspects of life. Today we see movies of women who were on the forefront of women's liberty in the 60's. Well if everything was so great for women back then, why did we need women to change what was going on?

Men supposedly had it made. The operative word is supposedly. Men had the burden of taking care of the family financially. Many worked themselves into an early death. It was a slap in a man's face if his wife had to go to work (even if she wanted to). He would be considered a loser.

The things we take for granted today were not available in the 50's and 60's. That made life simpler, but it sure is nice to be able to shop on the internet—take my wife—please. **Just kidding honey!!!!**

Sooo, what's so bad about today. Maybe we all should be more appreciative of today. If I had a time machine, I wouldn't want to go back living in the 60's. I like the women of today. I like working for a company that gives me paid vacations, paid holidays, health care benefits and 401K plans. None of those things were available for the average working person back then.

My feeling is when things are not going so good today; we always want to think people had it better in the past. The way we should be thinking, when things are not so good today, is they WILL be better in the future.

The future IS happiness

Felderstein—Kenny Felderstein

BLOG# 5

Three Is A Charm

She was at my son's bar mitzvah with a friend, but I didn't know it. She was at a reunion with my friend from Washington DC, but I didn't know it.

I first realized her at a friend's dinner at the Great Greek restaurant. I was going through my second ugly divorce. I was off of all relationships. I was writing my first book which was my only priority. She was with a friend of mine. Their relationship was just friends. She remembered me—I thought it was the first time I saw her.

The two divorces had cost me all of my money and a friendship with my oldest son; however I was very interested in her. I asked my friend Howard if she was available. He made it very clear that the two of us would never work. I didn't disagree, but I was interested. I went home that night to continue working on my book.

I couldn't get anything done because all I was thinking about was her.

The next day my friends wanted me to come to a party that night. I really wanted to work on my book, but before I said no, I asked Jay if Ellen would be there. He said yes and told me to meet at Howard's house so we could all go in one car.

There was no room in the car for all of us, so I asked Ellen if she would sit on my lap—she said: "OK." Driving to the party I said to Ellen: "I would like to take you out on a formal date." She said: "OK."

At the party, a slow song came on. I asked Ellen if she would like to dance with me (we Philadelphia boys and Jersey girls know how to dance). Ellen said: "OK." She and I were dancing very closely and when the slow song was over a fast song came on. During the fast song Ellen and I were still hip locked and dancing slowly.

On the ride back to Howard's house, I asked Ellen if she wanted to stay overnight with me. She lived an hour away and I was ten minutes from Howards' house. Ellen said: "OK." Then it dawned on me that I was a broke bachelor who only had one set of sheets and pillow cases plus three towels. I went into Howard's house and asked him if I could borrow a set of sheets and a few towels. He asked me why and I told him about Ellen staying over. Howard in shock, said: "you have got to be kidding me—this will never work."

On the way to my car, I remembered a line from Annie Hall and said to Ellen "Listen, when I get to my place I'm going to be a nervous wreck so please kiss me now before we get there—Ellen said: "OK."

Ellen and I are just about to have our 23rd wedding anniversary (together 27 years). She is the love of my life and the best thing that has ever happened to me. I know she loves me the same.

THREE IS A CHARM

BLOG# 6

Stop And Smell The Roses

Life is flying by so fast we forget to stop and smell the roses.

Appreciation is a big part of happiness. However, who has time to appreciate? There are so many negative things going on, I don't have time to stop and smell the roses. My job is so busy and stressful; I don't have time to appreciate. My spouse and kids are on me all the time and that leaves me no energy to stop and smell the roses.

Is that the way you feel? I know I did years ago. How can you get the happiness you deserve if you're not willing to take the time to appreciate the things around you? How can you get the happiness you deserve if you're not willing to take the time to appreciate the accomplishments you have achieved? How can you get the happiness you deserve if you're not willing to take the time to appreciate the things about your job that you like? How can you get the happiness you deserve if you're not willing to take the time to appreciate your family and friends who love you and want you to be happy?

The simple answer is—you have to take the time. You have to stop and smell the roses every day. That's right—every day. Appreciation creates positive energy—positive energy begets positive energy. The more positive energy in your life the happier you will be.

Here are your everyday exercises:

1. During the day we all see things that are interesting, creative, stimulating, fun, positive and beautiful. However, we just pass them by.

   Starting today, take a step back and appreciate what you're seeing or hearing. It might be for only a moment or an hour. The amount of time is not important, it's the taking it in and appreciating it.

   What you see or hear is also not important. It could be just the smile on a co-worker's face, the scenery on your way to work, the lunch you just had, an ad in the paper, a hug from the kids in the morning or one of my blogs (had to get a plug in there). I assume you get the idea.

What's important is that every day there is something to appreciate. Sooo, stop and smell the roses.

2. When you get home from work, the first person you see (wife, friend, family, etc.) say something positive. No matter how bad the day was, say something positive. It could be the roses you saw that day. If the only thing that was good that day was your lunch, the first words out of your mouth are to tell them about your great ham sandwich.

   If they say something negative back to you, take one of these three choices:

   One, ignore what they say and continue talking about something positive. Two, say to them, hey, I know you had a bad day, but something good must have happened today. Tell me about that. Three, leave and go on to the next person.

   This is YOU being the source of positive energy. Everybody likes people who are full of positive energy. Nobody "should" like people who are all about negative energy (however, some like to live in the negative). Remember, positive energy begets positive energy—negative energy begets negative energy.

3. For a least a month, stay away from negative energy. No reading negative news in the morning paper, no watching negative programming on the TV, stay away from negative friends and/or family, and no reading negative blogs (again, I just could not help myself promoting my positive blogs).

4. When you go to bed, lie on your pillow and before you fall asleep, think about at least two things you appreciate about your life, your family, your accomplishments, your job, or at least the money your job gives so you can have the good stuff you have. I am sure you can come up with at least two things you appreciate about your life.

You have to do these exercises every day. Don't skip a day. If you stay with it, I assure you will be happier than before you started these exercises.

Happier is a good thing. Appreciation leads to happiness. Sooo,

STOP AND SMELL THE ROSES.

BLOG# 7

Pets And Happiness

Man's best friend is ***not*** a dog. However a pet can be a "true friend." In my opinion, many of us should have a pet that makes us happy. The problem is—are you ready for the commitment?

Our dog, Zita, was named after my wife's aunt Zita. I named her Zita even though I never met the real Zita. The reason I did so was because my wife's entire family loved Zita—she was a true "loved one." Zita was a rescue dog that needed a lot of love. Naming her after a "loved one" allowed us to see her in a loving way.

Zita (our dog) is a "true friend" because she has delivered on the three most important elements of a "true friend." She is there for us. When we come home, she is waiting for us with her tail wagging trying so hard to give us a big kiss. When my wife had an operation she knew something was wrong and stayed by her side.

If someone tried to hurt us, Zita would risk her life to protect us.

Zita wishes us well and wants us to be happy. When she sees us sad, she seems depressed. When she sees us happy, she is full of excitement and wants to play. Lastly, she is the source of positive energy. She wants us to be happy because it makes her happy. She is never negative (unless we are negative). When we are down, being able to hug her brings us up. Zita, by all definitions is a true friend.

Zita is very smart, but the truth is that even the smartest dog is no smarter than a 3 year old child. If you ever had or took care of a three year old child you know it's a big commitment. Having any pet is a commitment. My wife and I can't run off to Las Vegas when we want. We have to plan ahead to make sure Zita is taken care of. We have to be available if she gets sick. We have to walk, feed and play with her. Is she easier to care for than a 3 year old human child—yes! However, loving her is a commitment.

The answer to the commitment problem is—am I getting back more than I'm giving? Does my pet make me happy? Am I getting positive energy from my pet? By the way, you can ask the same questions about your 3 year old human child. If the answer to these questions is YES, your commitment problem is solved. My wife and I are happy to commit to Zita.

If the answer to the above questions is NO, you are committed whether you like it or not. Deciding to have a pet or a child is a commitment you make before they arrive. You won't know the answers to the above questions before they arrive. It could go either way (YES or NO). Sooo, like it or not, unless you are a heartless soul, you are committed.

Are you ready for that? If not, don't get a pet or have a child.

What if the answer is NO? My blogs are about happiness. As I stated in other blogs, finding happiness, in a not so happy situation, is critical to your happiness. I stated, if you're not happy with your job, see it as a means to an end. If you're not happy in your relationship, make a change or focus on the parts of the relationship that make you happy. If you're not happy with your financial situation, remember "you will always have food to eat, air to breathe, and shelter—everything else is cosmetic."

Focus on your happiness, not on the things that make you unhappy. Focusing on the negative will never make you happy. If your pet (or child) makes you unhappy, focus on the other things in your life that do make you happy. You *are* committed to make the best of a bad situation. The more you find ways to focus on the things that make you happy, the happier you will become. The more you're happy, the more positive energy will be in your life. The more positive energy in your life, the happier you will become.

Happiness begets happiness. Positive energy begets positive energy. Be the source of positive energy by loving your pet.

BLOG# 8

Take This Job And Shove It

Does your job make you happy or unhappy? I'm about to tell you your job can make you happy even if you hate what you're doing. I'll bet that got your attention!

It's simple. You have the *control* to view your job as the "end" or a "means to an end." By doing so, you will only focus on the happiness you get from your job. By not doing so, you will only focus on the whole or parts of the job that makes you unhappy.

"What the hell am I talking about?" "How can I hate my job and still be happy?" Again, it's simple. If you love your job or at least parts of your job, you should view that as the "end." If you hate your job or major parts of your job then you need to use your job as a "means to an end." In both cases, "end" is happiness.

The trick is to have a "means to an end." That requires you to create something outside of work that leads to a happy ending (not that kind of happy ending). For example, if your family makes you happy then view your job as the entity that gives you the resources to enjoy your family. Those resources could be the money you make at the job, the travel you and your family get to do because of your job, the contacts and friends you and your family make because of your job, etc. etc. etc.

"Means to an end" might also be anything you love to do outside of work. It could be your hobby, playing the guitar, hanging out with your friends, taking cooking classes, creating a side job that makes you happy, etc. etc. etc. If you have those "outside of job" "endings," then you can look at your 9 to 5 as the entity that gives you the resources to enjoy those "endings." If you don't have those "endings," then your challenge is to create or find one or more.

Hating your job or even parts of your job will never lead to happiness. If you don't want to go through the risk of changing jobs then you have to look at your job with a smile on your face. Only focus on the parts of your job you like or the resources your job gives you outside of your job.

The "end" or a "means to an end" is a win-win situation. Being unhappy at your job is a lose-lose situation. You come home unhappy. You don't have the energy to create the "end" because you're depressed about your nine hours at the job. This negative energy will not only make you unhappy, it will affect your health, the people who love you, and your job.

That's right, being unhappy at your job will negatively affect your job. As you negatively affect your job, you start doing a bad job. That leads to more unhappiness and the possibility you'll get fired. Getting fired will make you and everyone else unhappy.

This chain of events is something you are able to control. It's simple, stop hating your job or parts of your job. Nobody is forcing you to hate your job—sooo, STOP IT!! If your job makes you happy, then it is the "end." If your job doesn't make you happy then remind yourself it's the "means to an end" that makes you happy.

Happiness leads to positive energy. Positive energy begets positive energy. Positive energy will have a positive effect on your life. Positive energy will make you, the people who love you and YOUR JOB better.

Your unhappy job will get less unhappy if you give positive energy to your job

BLOG# 9

Being Spontaneous Will Make You Happy

You're never going to create all the happiness you deserve if you don't have spontaneity in your life.

Being a spontaneous person doesn't mean you're a flake. You just can't have a life where everything is structured, organized and controlled. My life was like that. My administrator knew where I was every moment of the day. My life was like a gong, it went off and I was supposed to be at a certain place. When a window of time opened up she would fill it in with another commitment.

My personal life was the same. We ate the same things each day (Monday was hamburger day, Tuesday was chicken day, etc.), Saturday was movie day; sex was one way, never met new friends, never tried a new restaurant, etc., etc., etc.

Now, when I go on vacation, I don't wake up to an alarm. One of the first rules of vacation should be to never wake up to an alarm. When I wake up I wake up. So if I miss the helicopter ride, too bad, I slept. When I travel out of the United States, I always bring back the currency of that country. Why do I do that? Because, I believe I am going to go back again. I might not, but I believe I will.

I have money from Cairo. I don't know if I'm ever going to go back to Cairo, but I believe I will if I want too. Therefore, I don't have to see all of Cairo in one trip. I don't have to have every minute of every day scheduled because I'm afraid I'll never return.

When we went to Rome we only experienced less than half of Rome. We saw some wonderful, fantastic things. There weren't enough days to see it all unless we spent less time seeing the Vatican, Sistine Chapel and the Coliseum. We could have gotten to every place in Rome in the four days we were there. However, we only saw less than half of Rome because we wanted to just lay around in our beautiful hotel, have drinks, people watch at an outdoor cafe, spend an entire afternoon at the Vatican (you really need a week to see it all), etc.

The bottom line is we didn't view this trip as a onetime shot where we had to get everything in because we may never return. By doing so, we could be spontaneous and do what we wanted each day. Being spontaneous made the trip a very happy journey. BTW, we have vacationed in Rome many times since and have still not seen it all.

So, having a life of spontaneity is critical and important for you to be able to get all the happiness you deserve. I'm serious, you will never have all the happiness you deserve if your life is totally scheduled. You have got to get in tune with yourself. You have to find out what makes you happy. Being spontaneous will help you do that.

Now, let me give you the bad news. Commitment creates a spontaneity drain. Commitment sucks the life out of spontaneity. I'm not telling you to never make commitments. What I am telling you is you need to recognize the impact commitment has on your spontaneity and therefore your happiness.

What is commitment? If you have children the spontaneity in your life goes away. If you have a dog you give up a certain amount of spontaneity. I could cope with Dweezel, who was our cat, because at least we could leave the sucker for three days and go to Vegas. We just put enough litter and food down and he was actually friendlier when we would come home.

Both Ellen and I love dogs, so we rescued Zita. However, she takes spontaneity away from our life. If you buy a new car you have given up some spontaneity to make the car payments. Again, I'm not telling you don't buy cars, don't have kids, and don't have pets. What I am saying is, rationalize in your head how much spontaneity you are willing to give up for that commitment.

That new car feels good now and it's nice and shiny, but after a while you realize it's a piece of pretty iron that gets you to work and play. If you're paying $500 a month for your new car that's taking $500 a month from something you could be doing that is more spontaneous.

Sooo, just think about every one of the commitments you make in life. Remind yourself you are giving up something that is very, very precious to you which is called spontaneity.

BLOG# 10

People Don't Find The Happiness They Deserve For Four Main Reasons:

1. They don't know what they want.

2. Fear of failure stops them from making decisions and making changes.

3. Addiction (instead of preference) to money, ego and power stops them from their focus on happiness.

4. Pressures and expectations created by the outside world (your spouse, your friends, your boss, your commitments, etc.) becomes the reason you're not happy.

This blog covers reason one—**"People don't know what they want."** Future blogs will cover the other reasons.

People just don't focus on what they want out of a job, life and relationships. They just go through life not realizing how they got there. They wind up frustrated and unhappy not knowing how it all happened. Not being introspective, not taking a step back to evaluate where they are now, not thinking how they can change, and unwilling to change their lives because they're afraid of the consequences, leads them to the unhappiness state they're in.

When asked why they became a lawyer they reply: "well my mother was a lawyer." When asked: "why did you get married" they say: "It was time, my girlfriend wanted to get married, all my friends are married or my parents wanted grandchildren." When asked: "why did you take this job," they say: "security, money, a promotion, the power to control, my dad worked for this company or it was the only job I could get." When asked: "why do you stay with this friend or wife/girlfriend," they say: "it's hard meeting new friends, my parents and friends like her, I'm not sure I can do better, I would have to leave the neighborhood to find new friends, my wife/girlfriend may be a pain in the ass, but the sex is great or I can live with it because changing it will be too painful."

STOP!!!! This is YOUR life. It's not your parents, friends, bosses, wives, or girlfriend's life. What do YOU want? Do you want to go through life settling and accepting what the outside world gives you?

NOW is the time to collect your thoughts and be clear what you want. If you're not happy in your job—YOU can change it. Why take a promotion that will not make you happy? Why be in a profession that will not make you happy? Why work for a boss or organization that makes you unhappy? If you know what kind of job you want, go for it (as long as it is reasonable and doable). You may have to turn down a promotion, ask for a transfer to a different department, change careers and start at a lower level, take less money and lower your ego."

I was a senior executive in a job I hated. I asked for a transfer to marketing (my first love). My boss said; "Kenny, there isn't a senior job in marketing. You'll have to take a demotion. You probably will have to take less money. You're going to replace me when I move on so why would you want to do this?" I said: "because I'm not happy doing this job." Then I asked him: "are you happy doing your job?" He said: "I don't have to be happy. The money is good, my wife likes nice things. I'm not going to tell my family and friends I took a step down because I was unhappy."

That's when I realized my transfer request was right. I didn't want to be like him. The people (wife, friends, and family) who loved me wanted me to be happy. If they didn't, then I needed to let them go. I took the demotion and went to marketing. I loved my job and my boss. Eventually, I wound up running marketing.

Now is the time to look at your personal relationships with wife, girlfriend, friends, and family. My blog, "Three is a charm," tells how I went through two difficult divorces to find my love Ellen. We are together 27 years and they are the best years of my life.

If you're not happy with your wife, friends, or family, YOU can change it. Yes, it will be difficult. Yes, it will be an emotional disaster for both you and them. Yes, you will lose some friendships and some people will hate you. I had all those things happen to me. I survived. In time, my life got better. People that I never thought of as dear friends, became my best friends. The people who loved me knew I was not happy and they wanted me to be happy. My kids, who were upset, at the time, made great lives for themselves.

I'm not just talking about divorcing your wife. The same problems can happen when you leave your girlfriend, friends and family members. What good is it to have these people in your life if YOU are not happy? Life is so short. Before you know it, life will pass you by. I hope there is something more after this life, but we don't know for sure. This might be all we are going

to get. Please make the most of it. Don't go through life unhappy because you don't want to deal with the problems change will cause.
Life is great if you live it.

If you know what you want, you will get all the happiness that is available to you because:

YOU DESERVE IT!!!!!

BLOG# 11

The Second Reason People Have Trouble Finding Happiness:

"Fear Of Failure Stops Them From Making Decisions And Making Changes."

What is this fear of failure? Why, to some degree, do we all have it? How do I deal with this fear of failure and be OK making major decisions and major changes that will lead me to happiness?

What is this fear of failure?

Fear of failure is not a today thing, it's a future thing. We worry about making decisions or changes today because we don't know how it will affect us in the future. What if I decide to change jobs? Will I be successful? Will it make me happier? How will it affect my family and friends? If it doesn't work out, will the people who love me still love me? The same questions and concerns come into our heads if we make social decisions (like divorce) or business decisions.

The first thing I ask the people I mentor is: "what is the worst thing that could happen if you make this decision or this change?" Let's look at the future concerns stated above. What is the worst thing that might happen if your decision/change is not successful? Don't you trust yourself? Are going to put all of your effort to make it successful? You are the odds on favorite to make this a success. However, what if you're not?

One thing I can assure you of is: "you will always have food to eat, air to breath and shelter—everything else is cosmetic." Let me state that again: "you will always have food to eat, air to breath and shelter—everything else is cosmetic."

How can I make that guarantee? Are you a legal citizen? Are you able to work? Do you have an education? If the answer is yes to those questions, then "you will always have food to eat, air to breath and shelter—everything else is cosmetic." When I go to Home Depot I see people who are not legal in this country and don't have an education. They're standing outside talking to and, many times, having fun with their friends while waiting for someone to give them a days' work.

They're not rich nor do they have many of the cosmetic things we take for granted, but they do have food to eat, air to breath, and shelter. They would like a better life, but they have friends and family who love them. Many of them are happy with the little they have—"everything else is cosmetic." Therefore, if your decision or change is unsuccessful, YOU will survive, recover and make a better life for yourself.

Will this change or decision make me happier?

Well, you're not happy now! If you were, you wouldn't be making a major decision or change that you believe will make you happier. Sooo, what do you have to lose, take a risk, make that change, and/or make that decision. The worst that can happen is you'll stay as unhappy as you are now.

Always believe you will survive—you won't die. Believe you will recover and make other changes and/or decisions that will eventually lead to happiness.

How will it affect my family and friends?

I truly believe that when you're happy the people around you are happy—positive energy begets positive energy. When you're unhappy the people around you are unhappy—negative energy begets negative energy.

Be the source of positive energy. Focus on YOUR happiness first. Love yourself just a little more than anything or any person in your life. My mother would call that attitude—selfish. However, what I've learned in life is when I'm happy I have so much more to give to all the people around me. Giving makes me and them happy.

If it doesn't work out will the people who love me still love me?

This is when you really find out who wishes you well, who is your friend and who loves you. I hope all your decisions go as planned, but should they not, that's when you'll find out who is on your side. The people who love you love you just the way you are. The people who love you want you to be happy. Get rid of the ones that don't.

This is YOUR life not theirs. Living is not just getting through life. Living is getting the most out of life that is available to you. Your happiness is critical to having a great life. Decisions and changes are difficult and risky. The more right decisions and changes you make will make you happier. No decision or change will never lead to the happy life you deserve. Take the risk—go for it. What's the worst that can happen?

Why, to some degree, do we all have this fear of failure?

Your parents love you. They want you to be happy. Most of all, they want to protect you. Sooo, when you're growing up they say things like: "don't go into the street—you'll get hurt." "Don't put your hand in the fire you'll get burned." "Come to me for decisions because you are not old enough to make them."

To some of us they are saying you're not good enough to make decisions or do things on your own. Some parents push harder than others and some of us take it harder than others.

Also, many of our parents are scared to make decisions or changes. They got it from their parents. They go through life without focusing on their happiness. We watch the fear in them and some of us are affected by it more than others.

My parents put that fear of failure in me. They came through the early part of life when the great depression was happening. My father had a dead father and a sickly mother. He had to be the man of the family, at a young age, to support and protect his mother and three sisters. Living was really hard. Although he had food to eat, air to breath and shelter, every major decision was very scary. A NO decision was safer. He believed being happy was not the goal—survival was the goal.

I watched his fear and grew up with most of it inside me. He feared the future and I did also. I had no idea what the future would bring, but I feared it anyway. It took me years to truly understand that it was his fear, not mine. I have a choice. I can fear the future or I can accept that I don't know what will happen so why assume it will be bad. I can trust myself that if the worst happens I will recover, make new decisions and create a happier life.

I fought so hard trying not to be like him. I was angry with myself because I had this fear. Years later and with a great mentor, I realized the more I fought this fear the worse it became—"the more you resist the more he will insist." I had to accept that this fear is inside me. I didn't put it there, but it does exist. The issue is what I am going to do about it. I decided to take the risks in life that would make me happy.

Two divorces were painful, however like my other post, three is a charm. Ellen is the best thing that has ever happened to me. I made many difficult decisions in the business area. Some made me happier and some did not. I recovered from the ones that didn't and pushed on to a happier business life. I still have that fear of failure with me all the time; however it does not stop me from pushing toward a happier life.

Life is great. It's worth living if you decide to reach for the brass ring. Your happiness is in *your* control more than you think.

You just have to put your fear of failure aside and take the risks in life that give you what you deserve—HAPPINESS!!!

BLOG# 12

The Third Reason People Have Trouble Finding Happiness:

Their Addiction (Instead Of Preference) To Money, Security, Ego And Power.

The difference between an addiction and a preference is that an addiction is something you will never have enough. A preference is something you would like to have, but if you don't get it you're able to move on.

Everybody wants money. However, some people are addicted to it. Being addicted to money will require you to make decisions that will get you more money—not more happiness. I prefer to have money, but if I don't have more, I will live on what I have. I will always have food to eat, air to breathe and shelter. Everything else is cosmetic.

Everybody wants security. However, some people are addicted to it and because of that addiction, they stop taking risks, making decisions, and/or making changes that could lead to happiness. They often live in a self-defined box fearing to go outside because they might have to give up their security blanket. I prefer to have security (who wouldn't), but I'm not going to stop doing the things that might lead to my happiness because I'm fearful of impacting my security.

Everybody wants ego and power rewards. However, some people are addicted to it Being addicted to power and ego will never lead to happiness. You'll be defined by how the outside world sees you. You're addicted to the ego and power because you want "them" to believe you are "da man" (or "da woman").

My next blog will give insight into how being concerned by the outside world affects your happiness—read it. I prefer to have power and ego. It's nice to have the outside world look up to me. However, I love myself just the way I am. I don't need the outside world telling me I'm great—I know I'm great.

The purpose of ***money*** is the ability to shop till you drop—WRONG. The purpose of money is the ability to create security—WRONG. The purpose of money is the ability to have the outside world wish they were you—WRONG. The real purpose of money is CHOICE.

In a free and democratic society, having money gives you choices. You can choose to buy stuff. You can choose to keep it in the bank so you feel secure. You can choose to show the outside world how much money you have so they will look up to you. The more money you have the more opportunity you have to choose those things and many more.

The real issue here is will you make choices that lead to your happiness? If your goal is to make your happiness a lower priority than more money, that's the wrong choice. If you choose to not use your money for happiness so you can feel more secure, that's the wrong choice. If you choose to spend more money than you can afford so you look good to others, it's the wrong choice.

I prefer more money so I have more choices. I love my life just the way it is. If I hit the lottery, my first choice would be to help others who have fewer choices. My first choice wouldn't be to buy new cars, houses, and bling. My first choice would also not be to put most of it in the bank so I would never run out of it. Also, I would never use my new wealth to become something other than Kenny. Kenny is fabulous. People love Kenny. Why would I screw up the happiness I give others and they give to me just because I have more money? I'm Kenny and I will always be Kenny—rich or poor.

Don't get me wrong, I'm not one of those people who would give it all away. If I won enough money, I would buy new stuff and put enough away to feel secure, however that would not be my first choice because I'm happy with what I have now.

Security is a wild card when it comes to happiness. Everybody wants to feel secure. Everybody wants security for their family. However, addiction to security can get you to live your life in a way so that you don't put happiness as your first objective.

Most of us get the strong need for security from our parents. As we watch them struggle financially, we grow with this need to feel secure. If our parents were or are addicted to security, it got transferred into us. If our parents didn't use the money they had to build a happier life because they felt the money made them secure—we can wind up with the same problem. If our parents never left the box they created because the outside world was either too scary or might impact their security—we might create a box for ourselves.

If being secure truly makes you happy—I support that. If living in your self defined box truly makes you happy—I support that. However, make sure you're looking at your life without wearing blinders. It's easy to never take a risk, never make difficult decisions and/or make major changes. Not doing so will limit your risk to have a secure life. However, it may also limit the happiness that is available to you if you're willing to take a few baby steps outside your security zone.

Are you in a job you hate because it might impact your security if you make a change? Are you in a loveless marriage or relationship that does not make you happy because it might impact your security if you make a change? Are you not spending money and your time on doing something (like traveling, doing something creative, starting a side venture, etc.) that might make you happy because it might impact you and your family's security?

This is why security is a double edged sword. On the one edge we all want it. By feeling secure we feel happy. However, the other edge of the security sword could stop us from increasing the happiness within our reach. Life is too short, I choose to not let my strong desire to be totally secure affect my decisions, changes and risk taking. I'm not going to blow it all. I going to put some aside, but, I'm going to use what I can afford toward happiness. I don't want to spend the next years of my life being unhappy because I made every decision based upon security.

WHICH SIDE OF THE SWORD ARE YOU ON?

Addiction to ***power and ego*** will never lead to happiness. This is you living your life through the outside world. It's an empty happiness. You are trying to fill a void inside you with your need to have the outside world look up to you, envy you or be afraid of you.

You will never fill that void because an addiction, by definition, means you will never have enough. You will go through life trying to fill a never ending hole in your mind. Your focus will be on your addiction not on your happiness. JFK was asked: "mister president, why do you wear off the rack suits?" JFK said: "when you *are* the president, you don't have to look like the president."

If you are confident in whom you are, you don't need the outside world to tell you you're great and powerful.

BLOG# 13

The Fourth Reason People Have Trouble Finding Happiness:

Is Your Happiness Determined By The Outside World?

Who is the outside world? It's everybody and everything that is NOT you. Your spouse, kids, friends, family, neighbors, bartender, car, house, briefcase, etc. etc. etc. are the outside world.

Is the outside world bad? That depends on you. Do you make happiness decisions based upon how the outside world will react? Do you avoid changes because you believe the outside world might not approve? Do you avoid taking risks because "they" will think you're stupid? Do you need the outside world to tell you you're good enough? Do you need the outside world to make you happy?

All of us have some level of insecurity inside. Some have a lot more than others. Insecurity is a happiness killer. Insecurity gets you to think about the outside world consequences before you act. Insecurity is a hole inside you that some believe the outside world will fill. Insecurity will take away your control and give it to "them."

At 39 I went to a therapist. Bob was the one that got me to "see" how I was impacting my happiness ("seeing" is the topic of my next blog).

The first thing Bob said when I met him was: "Kenny, why are you here?' I responded: "I wouldn't need to be here if everyone would stop treating me in a way that makes me unhappy." Bob said: "I'm glad you came."

It took me a year before I understood how my statement was affecting my happiness. I was a good person. I had great friends. I was a star at work. Yet, I needed the outside world to tell me how wonderful I was. If "they", in any way, disagreed with me or hinted I wasn't the great person I was, I would defend myself to the death.

Bob didn't take the insecurity out of me. I will live with it for the rest of my life. He did convince me of two things. One, by needing positive feedback from the outside world, I was giving up control of my happiness.

Two, if the outside world disagrees or doesn't like me, it's their problem not mine.

I tell the people I mentor a story:

John finds a quarter in his pocket and puts it into his hand and closes his fingers around it. He goes up to Sally and says: "Sally, I have a quarter in my hand." Sally says: "no you don't. You never have any money and you don't have any now." John goes into defense mode and says: "Sally, why are you being so mean. I know I have a quarter in my hand." Sally again screams: "NO." John again screams: "YES."

Then John starts to think: "maybe Sally is right. Maybe I thought I put the quarter in my hand but I didn't. Maybe I dropped it. Damn, I'm stupid. I lost my quarter."

John was me. Bob convinced me that if I was in control of my insecurity and the outside world, I could have said to Sally: "Sally, I know you don't believe I have a quarter in my hand, but that's your problem. I know I have a quarter, so let's go to the store and buy candy. Less insecure, less giving in to the outside world, less stressed out—MORE HAPPINESS.

It took me awhile to "see" the difference between the insecure person inside me and the person I know I am.

I try to always be the great me, but that other person is still with me to this day. The difference is I know he's in there. By knowing "he" exists my "me" is in control much more than him. My next blog will give you some insight into how to deal with him.

When asked by your friends: "where should we go to dinner tonight?" Do you say: "I don't know? Where do you guys want to go?" That statement is bullshit. You know what you want to eat, but you won't say it because the others might not like your suggestion and, in your mind, might therefore stop liking you.

Why not try another approach. When asked the same question, say: "I would like Mexican, however if you all want something else I'm willing to go along as long as it's not seafood or fish." I assure you your friends, family, spouse, kids, etc. will not stop loving you because you told them what you want. Most likely they would prefer someone to make a decision (some because they fear that if they say what "they" want, the outside world will stop liking them).

If you want sex from your spouse, ask for it. The worst your spouse could say is not tonight. Will your spouse think less of you because you asked? If she or he does, maybe this relationship is and has been in trouble.

When you go to buy a car, is the first thing that comes to your mind how you'll be looked upon by the outside world? I know BMW hopes so. Could you really buy a car or truck you love knowing that it might not look good to your neighbors, wife, kids, restaurant valet, etc. If not, you've just given up your happiness to "them."

How much bling will make "them," not you, happy? How much happier will "they," not you, be in your two thousand dollar suit instead one from a three day suit outlet? How many promotions that you really don't want will you take to make "them," not you, happy? What if you like the job you're in and don't need the added stress? Oh, I forgot, you have to take the promotion because that will make "them," not you, happy.

What are you telling your kids when you buy them toys they play with for a day and get bored the next? It becomes an expectation, but does it really make them happy? Oh, I get it, you brought them more toys than they need so "they" will like you. Get real, they already like you. You're their family. You give them food and shelter. One toy is enough.

Growing up poor was an advantage (believe it or not) when it came to toys. We kids made our own toys (board games, bottle caps so we could play a game called beeries, etc.)—that made us happy. Seeing something we created made us happy. Why does it have to be about

YOU? Don't just get them what they want because you believe they'll like you better. Get them something they can use to be creative. Coloring books, dominoes, Legos, etc. will make them happier than a five hundred dollar toy.

We live in the outside world, but we don't need to be controlled by it. The outside world will always disappoint you eventually. If you need "their" approval, you will always be unhappy. The outside world needs you happy because many of them are unhappy. Many of the people you know are living to get the outside world to like them. You will be their hero if you don't need the outside world. They will look up to you because you like yourself more then you need "them."

Please trust me on this because I've been there—done that. Requiring the outside world to make you happy just doesn't work. Just think how great it would be if you didn't *need* the outside world to make you happy. Just think how even greater it would be if, every once in a while, "they" did something that does make you happy.

WOW, what a big plus.

BLOG# 14

"Seeing" is Happiness

In my previous blogs I discuss how our addictions to money, security, power and ego negatively affect our happiness. My blogs also state; "expecting the outside world to make you happy will, in the long run, never work." The question is where are these addictions to counting on "them," coming from?

There are two things going on inside most of us. One is a negative energy person who never feels good enough. That person believes the future will be negative. That person doesn't focus on what you have accomplished; he focuses on what you have failed. She doesn't want you to take risks because she believes you will fail. He doesn't want you to make changes because he believes you will just make things worse. She doesn't want you to make decisions because she believes you'll make the wrong decision.

That person inside you worries about things that haven't even happened yet. My parents worried all the time. They always felt the future was something to be concerned about, not something to look forward to. I used to joke that if my parents hit the lottery they would start to believe they got a bogus ticket and really didn't win. I will say they got it honestly by growing up during the great depression.

Guess what, I got that negative energy person inside me from them. However, any of us can get that person by growing up with negative energy (not just from your parents), by being in a traumatic situation (like an accident, a fire, death of a loved one, etc.) or a DNA personally trait that is susceptible to the negative stuff going around all of us all the time.

The bottom line is, that negative person inside us is "created" at a young age not born with it inside us. We all have it to some degree. Many of us are not affected by this person and can go on to a happy life. Some of us don't get the happiness we deserve because of him. I was one of those people. I'll call this person "Negative."

The second person inside of us is someone who lives in the present. That person doesn't worry about the future because he knows we don't know shit about the future. Hell, we don't even know what's going to happen while we're reading or writing this blog. That person believes she is good enough. That person acknowledges his accomplishments. That person can take a risk, make a decision and make a change because she believes it will lead to happiness. I'll call that person "Positive."

For people like me, Negative controlled my life much of the time. I wasn't happy within myself and felt the outside world had to make me happy. I held back from creating my own happiness because I didn't believe I deserved it nor would I get it on my own. I started to believe that if I didn't do something soon, I was going to end up like my parents who just wanted to get through life, happy or not.

This realization scared me more than mister Negative. So, I pushed mister Positive to take some risks, make some decisions and make some changes. Some worked and some didn't, but I survived. Some were very painful (like two divorces), but I survived.

At the time I didn't realize there was two of me. I was just running scared. Too scared to take control of my happiness and yet too scared to not take control. At 39 I decided to see a therapist. Bob help me "see" the two people inside me. He also helped me understand the effects Negative was having on my happiness. He helped me "see" that positive energy begets positive energy and negative energy begets negative energy. He helped me become the source of positive energy.

Why is "seeing" so important? When you can "see" Negative acting out, you have a choice to make. You can let him take control of your life or you can take a step back and say to yourself: "Negative is the past. I'm the current and the future. I have a choice. I can believe his negative input or I can believe in myself and change things for the better. I can trust that I will make the right decisions/changes and even if they don't work out, I will survive, move on and make better decisions/changes later."

By "seeing" mister Negative and acknowledging mister Positive, I will always focus on MY happiness. Negative wants to stay in a small box because he believes that bad things will happen outside the box. Positive wants out of the box because it's stopping him from creating a happier life.

"Seeing" was the hardest thing I ever accomplished. It took me over a year to "see." The reason it's so hard is because Negative is insidious. He comes out when you don't expect it. She gives you a negative ZUTS (it means a sharp pain going through your body—I made the word up) when you try to do something different.

For example, you want to change jobs. Positive says that a different job will lead to happiness. However, before you can take action on a job change, Negative gives you a ZUTS and convinces you that you'll fail, the next job will be worse, you will get fired, and then you will lose your family, your money and die. That may be an extreme, but a ZUTS can be that bad. Because of the ZUTS you decide to stay in the job you hate.

Negative will never go away. You'll have to live with him for the rest of your life. He will continue to come out when you don't want him. You can't stop her. However, what you can do is accept her just the way she is. You can realize she is the negative past and you are the positive current and future.

The best way to deal with him is like trying to stop a horse that is running out of control because he got spooked. You have two choices with the horse. Option one; you can pull up on the reins as hard as you can. This option doesn't work. The harder you pull the more out of control the horse will become—"the more you resist the more he will insist." Option two: while the horse is running out of control, you stroke his main and talk softly into his ear. As you keep stroking and whispering, the horse will eventually slow down and stop. Option Two is the way to live your life.

Sooo, don't try to stop Negative from affecting your life. Instead "see" him for what he is and let Positive do his thing.

To this day I still get ZUTS from Negative. The difference is his negative energy doesn't last long. Many times it lasts for just a minute and then Positive takes control. For example: The guy behind you hits your car while you're stopped at a light. Negative is all over you saying that your car is ruined, the insurance will blame you, you should beat up the guy who hit you, etc. etc. If Negative controls your thoughts you'll be upset for days—maybe even weeks.

If you can "see" Negative acting out, in less than a minute, Positive comes out and thinks: "no sense in getting all worked up about this. No matter how mad I am at this guy, I still have to get my car fixed. It makes no sense for me to worry about what may happen because I don't know shit about what is going to happen. What I do know is I need to get the information from this guy, call the insurance company, get my car fixed and move on."

Negative will spend days being angry—angry is negative energy. Positive will be over it before he gets home—less stress is positive energy.

I choose to accept mister Negative, but not be controlled by him. I choose to focus on mister Positive because he gives me positive energy. Positive energy makes me happy.

BLOG# 15

Sex and Happiness

Orgasms make me happy. I wish every person could have one or more orgasms. Some people think an orgasm is over-rated. I say, have two and call me in the morning. Some say hugging and kissing is more important than having an orgasm. I say, hugging and kissing is great, however an orgasm is fantastic.

Having great sex includes hugging and kissing, but the orgasm is the conclusion. Without it you usually feel unfulfilled. You can end the session without the conclusion, but it's a hell of a lot better if you end it with an earth shattering orgasm.

Some say foreplay is more enjoyable than the orgasm. I agree as long as the foreplay is more than hugging and kissing. The body has many erotic points. Foreplay that explores as many of those points as possible is a wonderful thing. However, erotic foreplay with someone you care for has to lead to a conclusion. Orgasm is the conclusion. It might not be as important as the foreplay, but without the conclusion of an orgasm, the body aches for a release.

Do you have to be in love to have great sex—absolutely not! That's a myth put into our heads by our parents and/or church. Sex can just be a happy and fun time with a person you care about. Making it more than it has to be, can ruin a great time.

If you are not having great sex it's either because you're with someone you don't care for or you're putting so much pressure on the fact that the sex has to mean something big. Stop believing sex has to be a deep emotional love event. Just go with the flow and enjoy it for what it is—fun and happiness. If it includes love great, but don't make it mandatory.

What makes me even happier than my own orgasm is when the person I'm with has an orgasm. I believe it's the responsibility of each partner to find a way to please the other. Being willing to explore the person's entire body to give them the pleasure they deserve, is being the source of happiness.

Slam bam thank you ma'am is not enjoyable for either person. Racing to see who finishes first, is not happiness.

Yes, an orgasm feels good, but if you don't care about the person you're with, you might just as well masturbate. At least that way you'll never frustrate the other person and have to worry about safe sex.

There are many reasons why pleasing the other person makes sex very enjoyable to me. Here are a few:

First, the negative energy person inside me and many others tries very hard to convince me I'm not good enough. Even though I've taking control of him, it still feels great when the person I'm having sex with feels satisfied. That makes me feel good enough.

Second, I'm the source of positive energy. I do all I can do to help people put positive energy into their lives. My mentoring and blogging are just one way I do so. Pleasing another person is giving them positive energy. There are many ways to please another person (unconditional love, true friendship, etc.). Great sex is one where both parties get a lot of positive energy.

Foreplay and after play are much more fun when both parties are enjoying it equally.

Sooo, if you want to get all the happiness you deserve, add sex to your agenda. Don't get too emotional about it, just enjoy it. Sex should be fun.

Fun leads to happiness.
Happiness leads to positive energy.
Positive energy leads to more happiness—
The circle goes on and on.

BLOG# 16

Friends and Happiness

"My friend" is one of the most misused statements in all the languages around the world. The reason is people use the word "friend" as a catch all to anybody who is another human being they like.

I grew up in a poor neighborhood where "friend" meant something specific. To be clear let me break "friend" into four categories:

1. Loved ones

2. Friends

3. Acquaintances

4. People who will help your career and/or better your life.

Loved ones:

These are the people you love and who love you. The operative word here is "love." The problem is many people describe "love" in different ways.

Puppy love has a different meaning for young boys than girls. A boy thinks it's about sex or being with the hottest girl in school. A girl thinks it's about sex, but places more emphasis on being with someone who treats her better than their parents or the father she never had. However, boy or the girl, puppy love is all about hormones.

Spouse love can be different than relative love, love of your children or love of your pet. Falling in love is different than being in love. Many people confuse "loved ones" with "friends." ***What we all can agree on is giving love and getting love makes us happy.***

For me to separate "loved ones" from "friends" I have to give you my definition of "love." Love can start out as hormonal, a friendship that gets more serious or needing someone for security. Over time you go from starting to love to falling in love. In any of these cases, love has to mature over time.

I'm in love with my wife. We started out on hormones. We couldn't get enough of each other. After the first year

I realized she was my best friend (I'll discuss "friend" next). It's 27 years later and I'm as horny for her today as I was our first month together. However, in addition to my hormonal attraction to her, I want to be with her because she makes me happy.

She loves me just the way I am and I'm not easy to love sometimes. I love her just the way she is. Sure there are things I would like her to change, but the pluses far—far—far outweigh the minuses. I have many more minuses than her, but she still loves me just the way I am.

When we fight with each other the situation only lasts a very short time (like minutes) because we both know we love each other. Once you truly know you're in love with someone and they are in love with you, fighting is counterproductive. We're not ever going to leave one another. If Ellen is fighting with me it's never because she hates me. Ninety percent of the time it's because she's having a bad day or I pressed a negative button from her past or she doesn't feel good. She knows the same is true about me.

Once we get it out of our systems, we take a step back and realize it's never about us and therefore, after a few deep breaths, we know that both of us love each other and will always be there for each other. Once you accept that fact, the fight is over.

In love also means we never want the other to be unhappy. It's so much easier to say "I'm sorry" when you truly love the person you're fighting with. In love also means you appreciate each other. Ellen is my third wife. I thought I was in love with the other two, but after my years with Ellen, I realize I never loved them the way I love her. Many times I lay in bed looking at her sleeping and think how lucky I am.

I appreciate so many things about her and I know there are many things she appreciates about me. I love that everybody we meet want to be around her. I appreciate that she is the source of positive energy. She makes me want to be like her (positive energy begets positive energy).

Sooo, love is something that has to mature over time. All the things I mentioned as to why I'm in love with Ellen took time to be realized. Love knows the person will always be there for you. Love is feeling loved by the other person. Love believes you will always be together through good and bad times. Love is appreciating each other. Love is feeling positive energy from each other. Love is making each other happy.

A famous movie star, who had many options regarding women, was asked what his secret was to being with one woman for thirty years. He responded: "it's easy to be a good lover with one woman for a few months or a year;

however a great lover is one who can please (not just sex) a woman for her entire life.

If you want to read how my wife and I fell in love, read blog #5 "Three is a Charm."

Friends

Many of the aspects of love exists in a friendship, however you're not in love with a friend. A friend is someone who wishes you well and wants you to be happy. A friend is someone who you believe would be there for you in need. A friend is someone you enjoy hanging out with. A true friend makes you happy.

However, a friend is not a "loved one." When you're in love it's like the other person is part of you. A friend complements you. Friendship could last forever, but how many of us have had a friend who has disappointed us. How many of us have had a friend who left us or we left them.

Friendship can change over time. People go their own ways. True love, as described above, does not change over time. That's why true love needs to mature to a point so that it will not change over time.

For someone to become a "true" friend they have to pass the "wish you well—I'll be there for you" test. If they pass the test, they become a true friend. A true friend has to be someone who is full of positive energy. A negative energy person could be a friend, but should never be a true friend.

I have a few true friends. One of them, Mark, was a surprise. When I divorced my first wife, a few of my so called close friends left me. It was a shock to my system because these were people I grew up with and "believed" would always be there for me. Mark was not a close friend—he was just a friend. However, as soon as he heard I was leaving my wife, he called me and said: "Kenny, are you alright? I heard what is going on and I want you to know my wife Patty and I will not be taking sides. We want you to be happy and if we can do anything for you, let us know." At that moment, Mark (and Patty) became a true friend. Over thirty years have passed and we're still true friends.

A "true" friend can become a "loved one" (as it was with my Ellen). A friend, on the other hand, is just a friend that you "hope" will become a "true" friend over time. I have many friends and a few true friends. ***Having friends and true friends makes me very happy.***

Acquaintances

Too many people meet someone one or two times and call them a friend. An acquaintance is not a friend. You don't have any expectations that an acquaintance will be there for you, wishes you well or will make you happy. An acquaintance is just someone you met who might become a friend over time.

People who say they have a hundred friends are for sure counting acquaintances in that list. It's great to have as many acquaintances as possible. The reason is that some of them might become friends. The more friends you have the more chances some of them might become true friends which can lead to more loved ones. You're happy when you have friends, happier when you have true friends and the happiest when you have loved ones.

Therefore, collect as many acquaintances as possible, but stop calling them friends. Calling them friends diminishes the friends you do have.

People who will help your career and/or better your life

These are not people you meet—these are people you seek. It's important to seek out people who can help your career or better your life. As a Mentor, I'm someone a person, who is not happy, should seek. I can make that person's life better. There are other people who can help you with your career and your life. Find them. Everybody needs a little help in life. The more of these people in your life the better your life will become. The better your life becomes, the happier you become.

The best part is that some of these people might become an acquaintance, who then might become a friend, who then might become a true friend, who then might become a loved one. The more of these people you have in your life the happier you will become.

If you have a lot of loved ones, friends, acquaintances and people who help you, you're one of the lucky ones. Appreciate and cherish all of them.

BLOG# 17

Religion and Happiness

This blog is going to be controversial. Some of you might not agree with what I'm writing, however please have an open mind. All of my writings are my opinion. My purpose is to get you to look at your life, job and happiness through different eyes. My purpose is not to get all of you to agree with me. Remember the goal is happiness.

First, let me start by giving you ***my*** definition of religion. Religion, in my opinion, is *any* organization that is organized, has a set of rules or requests, has followers that, for the most part, follow those rules or requests, take in money to support the organization, have a single leader with sub leaders, might or might not worship an entity that only exists in the minds of the followers (God is an example, but not the only example) and their purpose is to give a better life for their members.

The reason I added that a religion may or may not worship an entity is because some true religions do not worship a supreme being.

Being religious, again, in my opinion, is someone who follows the religion, supports the religion, follows the rules or requests and makes religion a significant part of his life.

In my definition of religion, if you take away the non-tangible entity, almost any organization can be a religion. What I mean by non-tangible entity is someone you can't see or touch with our limited five senses. Therefore, it only exists in our minds and hearts.

With my definition, if you take away the non-tangible entity, could a corporation be a religion? A corporation is organized, has a set of rules and requests, has followers that follow those rules, takes in money (from profits) to support the corporation, has a single leader (CEO) and sub leaders (VPs, directors, managers). However, the corporation's purpose is not to give a better life for its employees. Its purpose is to make money which may or may not make the employees happy.

Under my definition, a Union could be a religion. However, nobody sees it as such because it doesn't have a spiritual nature to it. I have no idea what "a spiritual nature" means because I'm too logical and can't put my arms around it. Therefore, I can only assume that "a spiritual nature" is something a person feels inside.

I assume you can't really be a religious person unless you have a "spiritual nature" inside you.

OK, what the hell does all this have to do with happiness? Again, in my humble opinion (IMHO, yes, I text a lot), being part of a religion is a good thing. What I have a problem with (here comes the controversy) is being religious can retard your happiness.

The reason is that making one thing a big part of your life is restricting. Religion's rules are restricting. Having those rules as a significant part of your life means you're not creating your own rules of life. Not creating your own rules of life will not allow you to get all the happiness you deserve.

It's OK to believe in a non-tangible entity, however believing that entity will guide your life, believing that entity is making decisions for you, believing that entity will give you a better life, believing that entity will allow you to join him or her in the happier afterlife or believing if something good or bad happens to you or anybody else it's the entity's will, is putting the entity in control of *your* happiness.

If you're reading my blogs, you know I believe if you give control of your life to the outside world, you will never get all the happiness you deserve. You are the master of your happiness not them. Giving control to a non-tangible or tangible entity is giving control to the outside world.

If you join a religion for the purpose of community you will get a lot out of it. If you join a religion because you want to be guided by someone or something other than *you*, you will be missing a big chance to control your life. Some people think being controlled by something else is a good thing. I don't.

I'm a spiritual being not a religious being. I believe in giving positive energy out to the universe because I believe the more you give the more you get back. I'm not giving myself to the universe and being controlled by its whims. I'm making the universe a better place because I'm giving it *my* positive energy. Lastly, I believe being the source of positive energy to others will make my life happier.

If it makes you happy, join a religion. Just don't let the religion control your life and your happiness. Being spiritual will give you all the positive energy you need. Sooo, be spiritual not religious.

Again, this is my opinion. I hope you will be open minded to what I've written and not reject it out of hand because it is not the way you were brought up.

My only goal is your happiness. If your way makes you happy, do your thing—as long it's your decision not theirs.

BLOG# 18

A Beautiful Beach—Somewhere

There's a song that describes all kinds of not so nice things that happens to someone. They're minor things like, someone stealing that stool you were waiting for at the bar or waiting too long for the Doctor because the nurse forgot to tell him you were waiting. However, while these bad things are happening, instead of getting angry or frustrated, that person closes his eyes and pictures a beautiful beach somewhere.

I love this song. If only everyone would see life this way the drug companies would be out of business and everyone would be happy.

How do *you* feel about this song? Do you think it's possible to have an asshole with a road rage attitude, flip you the bird, and your reaction is:

A Beautiful Beach—Somewhere

If you do, you'll live longer.

Do you think it's possible to have someone, take the parking spot you've been waiting for and your reaction is:

A Beautiful Beach—Somewhere

If you do, you're one hell of a happy person.

Do you think it's possible to have your dentist start drilling before you're numb, and all you can think about is:

A Beautiful Beach—Somewhere

If you do, you get it. You're my hero. I want to be like you. You're the person I want to hang out with. You're the one who gives positive energy out to the universe. You're the least stressed person on the planet. You have many—many friends and loved ones. You make everyone around you feel better. You've been reading my blogs.

Wouldn't that be a great way to live! Sooo, why not? What's stopping you? What bad could happen to you—absolutely nothing!

It's hard to think like that. I, your happiness blogger, have not reached that pinnacle. I don't know anyone who sees life that way all the time. I can do it more times than not, but not all the time. The thing is I don't know why.

I know it would be good for me. I know I would be a happier person. I know everyone would like me even more than they do now—which is a lot. I want to be that person, but something is holding me back.

Are the wounds, inside me, from the negative things that happened in my life, so deep I just can't release them entirely? Probably so! Is the negative energy of not wanting to be taken advantage of so deep inside me I can't get rid of it? Probably so! Are my insecurities stopping me from taking a laissez faire attitude when things don't go my way? Probably so!

I'm working on it and I will continue to work on it the rest of my life because I know my life will be even better than it is today if I accomplish that goal.

Oh crap, the dog just took a dump on the living room floor

"A BEAUTIFUL BEACH—SOMEWHERE"

BLOG# 19

Giving the Universe Positive Energy Brings Happiness

Positive energy begets positive energy. If you've been reading my blogs you've read that a few times. I keep saying it because it's true. The people who are the source of positive energy are the people we all want to hang out with. The people who broadcast positive energy out to the universe are happy people.

The problem is in a world of negative energy how do you become the source of positive energy? It's not easy. It takes effort. It takes self-trust. It takes self-respect. It takes self-love. It means you have to love others unconditionally even if you don't get what you want. It means asking for what you want without demanding it. It means accepting what's happening to you now with the belief you will make it better in the future.

The hardest part of becoming the source of positive energy is it puts the responsibility on YOU. That means YOU don't get help from somebody or something which will make you a positive person. You have to believe your problems will get solved in a positive way—eventually. You have to get out of a negative energy spiral all by yourself. You have to believe the negative things in your life are not serving YOU. You have to be willing to make the changes needed to become a positive energy person. You have to believe you will always have food to eat, air to breath and shelter.

The way to start on your journey is to put positive energy into your life and stop surrounding yourself with negative energy. Here are a few suggestions to get you started:

- Stop reading, watching, and listening to negative news. The people who make antidepressant drugs hope you continue to dwell in the negative. The broadcasters believe negative news sells. The best way to stop them is to stop being an observer. I truly wish some rich person will create a positive news network. Probably won't happen because rich people have stock in pharmaceutical companies.

- Until you become the source of positive energy, end your relationship with negative energy people—all of them. That's right, your spouse, friends, coworkers, etc. have to go if they continue to pull you down with their negativism.

- See your job as a positive entity because it's either an "end" or a "means to an end."

- Everyday appreciate what you have and don't focus on what you don't have.

- Get new people into your life who gives positive energy out to the universe.

- READ MY BLOGS

I didn't say this would be easy. Negative forces are all around us and for some, within us. Only you can break the negative chain. What I will guarantee you (because I live it) is the more positive energy you give out to the universe the more positive energy you will get back. The more you continue to give out the more you get back. It goes on and on. It's called the positive energy spiral.

I do know living with negative energy never works. Sooo, stop it today and try what I'm suggesting—especially the part about READING MY BLOGS!!

BLOG# 20

Three Prescriptions To Happiness

Prescription One

"Three Prescriptions To Happiness" is a fabulous book by Ken Keyes Jr. The book changed my life and I suggest all of you read it. Don't just think about it, go out (or online) and get it today! The three prescriptions are very easy to read, but hard to execute. They are:

#1 "Ask for what you want, but don't demand it."

#2 "Accept what's happening for now."

#3 "Love unconditionally even if you don't get what you want."

Below is my interpretation of Keyes's prescription number one. My follow on blogs will cover prescriptions two and three. Again, this is my interpretation not yours. Read his book and see how his message could change your life.

#1 "Ask for what you want, but don't demand it."

How many times does someone ask you what you want and you say: "Oh, I'm not sure, what do *you* want?" For example, you're going out to dinner with friends and they ask you: "what would you like to eat tonight?" Is your response: "I don't care, what do you guys want to eat?"

YOU DO CARE WHAT YOU WANT TO EAT!! Not stating it is saying you don't think of yourself as someone who has an opinion. Not stating it is saying you don't think of yourself as someone who deserves a choice. You don't want to be controversial. You don't want your friends to not like you because you voiced your opinion. Why not say: "I would like Italian, but if everyone else wants something else, I'll go along with it—as long as it's not Indian food."

The friends who asked you the question want you to be happy. They might be people who don't like to make decisions. They probably will go to whatever restaurant you want.

Let me give you a true personal situation. I was taking my kids to a Chinese restaurant. I was going through my first divorce and was very sensitive to making my kids happy. It was Christmas time. The place was full except for the last table in the back. When we got to the table, I asked the kids which side of the table they wanted to sit. They said: "Dad we don't care."

If I sat on the seat to my left, I stared directly at a blank wall. If I sat on the seat to my right, I stared at the beautiful Christmas tree at the front of the restaurant.

Knowing this, I again asked the kids where they wanted to sit. They again said: "we don't care." Then it struck me—I wanted to sit on the right so I could see the beautiful Christmas tree. I didn't want to stare at a blank wall. I was paying for the dinner. The kids were just interested in the food. After I slapped myself in the head, I said to the kids: I would prefer to sit on the right so I could see the Christmas tree—is that OK with you guys." They said: "sure dad."

Sooo, ask for what you want, but don't demand it. You will get what you want more times than you think and you deserve it! Ask your spouse for sex—the worst he/she will say is not tonight and you'll say: "OK." Ask your boss for a raise—the worst he/she will say is no and you will say with a smile: "it didn't hurt to ask." Ask your friends to go to the Italian restaurant—the worst they will say is we don't want Italian and you will say: maybe next time—OK?"

Asking is good—demanding is bad. Demanding is stressful. Asking is less stressful. Demanding assumes you won't get what you want. People demand because they don't believe they deserve to get what they want. They get aggressive as a defense against their insecurities.

Asking assumes you might get what you want, but even if you don't your life will be just fine. Demanding will lose friends and loved ones. Asking will create more friends and loved ones.

The more you love yourself, the more you will get what you want—
YOU DESERVE IT!

BLOG# 21

Three Prescriptions To Happiness

Prescription Two

As stated above, below is my interpretation of Keyes's prescription number one. My follow on blogs will cover prescriptions two and three. Again, this is my interpretation not yours. Read his book and see how his message could change your life.

Prescription Two: "Accept what's happening for now."

This was the hardest prescription for me. During the difficult times in my life I found it hard to accept what was happening to me. I was so unhappy because all I could think about was "why me God?" I was frustrated because I couldn't control the negative things that were happening to me. I was pissed off at the people that were making me unhappy, scared and frustrated.

Then I read Ken Keyes's book and started to realize I was making myself miserable because I just couldn't accept what was happening to me. I wanted to control the uncontrollable. I wanted the people who were doing this to me to stop. Once I accepted (which took me a long time) what was happening to me for now, I could begin to think about what I could do (control) about it.

After my divorce, my youngest son became ill. He was living sixty miles from me and in a hospital. I was angry, frustrated and scared he would not recover. I was also upset he was sixty miles away from me. All of these feelings made me very unhappy.

By accepting what had happened and that I couldn't turn back the clock, I started to realize there were things I could do to help my son (and me) to get over it. First, I had to accept that his mother did not want this for him. She was angry at me for the divorce and I was angry at her. I needed to realize it would not serve me or my son if I stayed angry at her.

Second, I could make sure my son was in good hands and in the best facility I could afford. He was and they helped him get over his problem in six months. Today, he's a lawyer, a great husband, a great dad to my two grandchildren and a true friend of mine.

Three, I could limit my social life and drive the 60 miles to see him almost every day. He got better and our relationship became a bond. By not accepting, I was always unhappy and could only focus on what was happening not on what I could do about it. By accepting, I could focus on doing something about it. I was sad about what my son was going through, but happy that I was doing the best I could to help him.

Sooo, when things are not going the way you want, accept what's happening for now and focus on the things you could do about it now and in the future. It might take some sacrifice, but, in the long run, it will change the negative to a positive.

You have the power and control to make choices to affect your happiness. If you need to divorce your spouse, you probably will have to give up a lot (money, security, family being angry at you, etc.). However, will keeping your money, security, etc. make you happier than accepting a marriage that's making you very unhappy? The right answer is: if the marriage (or anything else) is holding you back from seeking happiness, take the steps, although painful, to change it.

Please, accept today and make the sacrifice to make yourself happy.
YOU DESERVE IT!!

BLOG# 22

Three Prescriptions To Happiness

Prescription Three

As stated above, below is my interpretation of Keyes's prescription number one. My follow on blogs will cover prescriptions two and three. Again, this is my interpretation not yours. Read his book and see how his message could change your life.

Prescription three: "Love unconditionally even if you don't get what you want"

Can you love your enemy? OK, probably not. Can you love a person who does not like you? It's possible. Can you love a person who disagrees with you? You should be able to at least do that. Can you love a person who likes you and agrees with you all the time? Yes.

Think of a world where everyone loves everybody. I know it won't happen in our lifetime. However, just think about it. There wouldn't be any enemies. There might be people who don't like you, but they would acknowledge, respect and accept you. There might be people who disagree with you, but still love you. That's the world I choose to live in.

Sooo, how do we create a world like that? It should start with you. If you wait for everybody else to start it, it will never happen. Can one person change the world? I believe it could happen. It's called "pay it forward."

Is it making me happier to hate the Taliban? I know most of them hate me (because I'm an American), but sitting at my PC and having hatred in my heart for all of them, will not make me happier.

My first and second wives put me near bankruptcy and I was mad at them for that. But, as I began to listen to the words of Ken Keyes, I started to realize that anger was not serving me. What if I could focus on the good things that happened in our marriages? What if I could love them just the way they are? Would my life get better or worse? Once I let the anger go, my life got better.

I have a true friend who disagrees with me and sometimes instigates a fight between my wife and me.

Kenny (believe it or not he has the same name) and I fight, but we love each other. We laugh together all the time. Once the fight is over, we do high fives and know that our friendship will last forever. Kenny believes in prescription number three.

I would like to think my positive energy and my lack of anger (even at people I don't like or have done me harm) has rubbed off on others. I would like to think the people I've touched understand that loving instead of hating makes them happier.

The outside world will not give you what you want all the time. Hating "them" or being angry at "them" never served me. I put myself in first position. I love myself just a little bit more than anybody or anything else in this world. I try my best to run my life in a way the makes me happy. Believing and conducting my life as Keyes suggests in prescription number three, makes me happy.

Try it!! Take the anger and hatred out of your life. Love your enemy or people that don't act the way you want. You'll feel better, your life will get better, and you'll be happier. Do it for ***you*** not for them.

If ***you*** try it, maybe someone else will try it. Then someone else will try it. Then someone else will try it. If enough people try it, we're on the way to a world where everyone loves everyone else.

That's the world I want my children and their children to live in, but it has to start with YOU!!!

BLOG# 23

Happiness Is Meeting New People

People like to do things in Packs. This was and is true in the animal world and the early human era. Even today we still form Packs with friends and family. Too many of us don't go outside the Pack to enhance our happiness.

A close Pack is comfortable. A close Pack makes us feel safe. A close Pack makes us feel wanted. A close Pack enables us to show more of ourselves. A close Pack usually has people in it who view the world politically, religiously and emotionally the same or near the same. A close Pack takes less effort.

Animals need a close Pack mainly for safety. Humans don't need a close Pack. We choose to form or be included in one for the reasons stated above. That choice limits our knowledge. That choice limits our understanding of different cultures, religions, politics, etc. That choice limits us from sharing our emotions and view of the world to all who will listen. That choice limits our happiness.

Last night I met three new people. Each of them had very interesting things to say about a variety of subjects. I learned more new things in a few hours with these people than I've learned from my "Pack" in the last two weeks. They on the other hand got to see me and my views which I believe was interesting to them.

We learned serious information and, once we became comfortable with each other, found many things to laugh about. I left the bar happier for the experience. Will I ever see these people again—maybe—maybe not? That's not the issue. Having new knowledge and a positive fun experience was the reward.

Happiness is not something given to you. Happiness is something you have to seek. Waiting for happiness never works in the long run. Making an effort to find or create happiness is our job if we want to get the most we deserve out of life.

Giving positive energy out to the universe and getting positive energy back will make us happy. Making an effort to meet new people who you can share your knowledge and positive energy and get some of it back, is a great way to enhance your happiness.

Some of you will say meeting new people can be boring. I say, maybe you're not asking the right questions. Maybe you're not sharing your true emotions and beliefs to the new people you meet. Maybe you're not listening because those people aren't saying what you want to hear.

A boring party is only so if you make it so. If you're willing to be "out there" with the crowd, I assure you the party won't be boring and you'll probably meet new people who will enhance your knowledge and happiness.

Showing yourself to people you never met before can be scary, but with no risk there is no reward. Always ask yourself "what's the worst that can happen?" I say the worst that can happen is this new person will never talk to you again. So what!! You still have your Pack to go back to.

Letting people see you as you are is fulfilling. Doing so to only your Pack is reducing your potential for happiness to a handful of people.

Sooo, get your ass out there and go to any place where you have the chance to meet new people. When you meet them, don't hold back. Let them have all of you. Don't do it for them, do it for you. I promise you and they will have a great time.

Remember, the more you resist the more they will resist. The more you expose yourself and your beliefs the more they will expose themselves. This give and get will bring more happiness to everyone.

BLOG# 24

Happiness, Some Things To Think About

While going through my metamorphosis from unhappy to happy, I found some writings that helped me through. Some, I wrote. Some, others wrote. Here are a few:

Regarding the importance of appreciation in regard to happiness, I, in my own words, wrote (in my first book "Never Buy a Hat If Your Feet Are Cold—Taking Charge of Your Career and Your Life) about a story Ken Keyes Jr. wrote in his book "Handbook to Higher Consciences (another great book from Keyes you should read):"

"*A guy, in Africa, is being chased by tigers. He's running like hell to get away from the tigers when he finds himself at the edge of a cliff. The tigers are coming at him. He looks down the cliff and sees a vine that goes from the top to the bottom. He starts to shimmy his way down the vine. He gets half way down, looks up and there are those tigers sitting there waiting for him. Then he looks down and, guess what, more tigers down below.*

There he is, mid-way down the cliff. He has tigers up above and more tigers down below. He looks straight ahead and sees a strawberry bush growing right out of the cliff. He plucks one of the strawberries and eats it. It is the best strawberry he has ever had."

If your life is tigers up above and tigers down below, always remember there are strawberries right in front of you that are delicious. Take the time to appreciate them. I would encourage you to appreciate the things you have in life and focus on them. Not just appreciate them but focus on them.

Regarding the effects of "Fear of Failure" on happiness, a friend of mine, Mike Bemiss, wrote "***Beware of the Known:***"

"It is not the unknown we must fear. As children everything was unknown. But as we get older we start to build walls around ourselves at the limits of what we know. We build the walls of our own jail because we fear failing at doing something unknown. Too soon we build a castle of security

around ourselves. It has no doors and few windows, it is the known.

We live and die in there with only an occasional timid peak out a high window at the unknown. We build the walls of our known so high that we cannot escape, but our souls wither and die with lack of new experiences. I refuse to build that wall. Each stone I use to build it, I will use instead as a stepping stone into a new and different unknown. And when I die, as we all do eventually, my only regret will be that I never got to discover the next unknown.

I appreciate the known, but I refuse to be limited by it. It can be a trap if you let it and you will never experience the next unknown which is the most special unknown of all, the next one."

Fear of failure stops you from making decisions. It stops you from making changes. Most of all fear of failure stops you from taking risks. Risk taking is the unknown. Take some risks. You'll be surprised at how good the unknown can feel.

Being afraid of failure is never going to lead to happiness. No risk taking is safe. Risk taking will lead to happiness. Sooo, take a risk. You will survive even if it doesn't go your way.

Lastly, when I managed a district of salespeople, I attached a card to their phone (landline phone—cell phones were not invented then—shit am I old). The saying I created on the card said:

"Is what I'm doing or about to do getting me closer to my objective."

I wanted my salespeople to think about that before they made a call to their customer or supplier. What I realized later was that saying was a good way to run my life.

Every day we do things that have nothing to do with our objective. One reason for that is we don't know what our objective is. The one I focused on was happiness. *Is what I'm doing or about to do getting me closer to my happiness?*

You can have more than one objective, but remember, there is only one number one objective, one number two objective, one number three objective, etc. etc. etc.

Focus on the one that will make you the happiest.

BLOG# 25

Happiness In The Future

Today is today—tomorrow is tomorrow. What you do today doesn't mean you'll be doing the same in the future. BTW, future does not have to mean many years from now. It could mean weeks or months from now.

Many things you do today are out of need (like making a living) or out of responsibility (like taking care of children, mom/dad, etc.). However, many things you do today are because you don't know any better.

Now is the time to think about a time when you'll be able to do the things you think will make you happier. I suggest you take a piece of paper and draw a "T." On the left side top of the "T" write "Today." On the right side top of the "T" write Future.

Under "Today" write down all the things you do today. An example could be:

- Work as an accountant eight hours a day
- Take care of my dog
- Spend time with my friends and family
- Date once in a while

Under "Future" write down the things you're capable doing in the future that will make you happier. Remember, the future could be weeks or years from now. Don't write down things you would like to do if you hit the lottery. Be realistic. An Example could be:

- Change jobs and go into sales
- Take care of my dog
- Spend time with my friends and family
- Get into a committed relationship
- Do something creative, like painting

Every one of the "Future" list has to be realistic. The best way to change jobs is to start doing something on the side while you maintain your current job. The only thing that stops you from testing the waters on selling is your time. If you're willing to use your time, after your day job, to sell something, you have the control to do so.

I'm not saying getting a full time sales job at a major company while you still have your day job is realistic. What I am saying is you can keep your current job and sell, at night, web adds, Mary Kay products, etc. etc. You can do the same if you want to become a marketer or any work related job that makes you happy and can be done after your day job.

If what you want to do require training, you have the control to go to school at night. It's all about your time and how you spend it. After you have experienced the job you believe will make you happier, you will then know if it lives up to your expectations of happiness. It might or it might not. If it does, then work at it until you feel comfortable switching from you're not so happy job to the happier one.

Start now. Don't wait for the future to happen. Make the future happen a little bit at a time. Slow and steady does win the race.

You're not in complete control of getting into a committed relationship. However, if you wait for someone to show up, it won't happen. You do have control of the time available to you. Use that time to meet people. Go to or get involved in religious functions, community functions, political functions, etc. etc.

BTW, you can also go to upper end bars to meet professional people (professional does not mean rich. It means someone who is professional in whatever job they do). Kenny (oh that guy again—my true friend the instigator) and I go to Wolfgangs in Beverly Hills twice a week. We have met a lot of people and have a fun time. Some of them have become friends. If I were single, I would choose Wolfgangs over the Internet to find someone who I could spend my life with.

Start today. Get out there and meet people. The more people you meet the higher the chance you will meet your committed relationship partner. Waiting for the future to bring someone to you will not work.

You're in control of doing something creative. You don't have to be great at it—you just have to enjoy it. The two most important elements in doing something creative are:

1. Something you are willing to spend your time doing because it makes you happy

2. Do it for *you* not the money or anybody else.

If you follow those two simple rules, you will be happy doing something creative even if you stink at it.

Start today. Try doing something creative. You may love it or hate it, but you'll never know if you don't try. Who knows, you may be good at it and that could replace your not so happy job.

Ok, what about me. I do the "T" thing all the time. I started at 39. My "Future" list included:

- Mentor people using my life experiences. I tell my peeps that a Mentor is different than a Therapist. A Therapist is book trained. The books he obtained his information from are great writings from some very knowledgeable people. However, the Therapist has not lived it. A Mentor is life trained.

- I've had and still do have a very interesting life. I've had the thrill of victory and the agony of defeat. If you have read my blogs you know some of the situations I've lived through. By living it, I can relate to the people I'm mentoring..

- I started mentoring people on business at 22 when I first became a manager. I didn't wait for the future. I wanted to do it because it made me happy. After experiencing the life I've had and still have, I now have many other things (other than business) I can help people with.

- Lecturing to groups of people makes me happy. I love to be in front of an audience. In high school I sang on stage at my Prom. In business I was the one they always wanted to present to the senior managers and new hires.

- I thought I would become a world renowned lecturer. At 39, while keeping my day job, I started lecturing to night class groups, Universities and a boat cruise on "Taking Charge of Your Career and Your Life."

- I'm very good at it; however I found out that making a living at lecturing is very rare. After studying it for some time, I realized that lecturing was show business. Show business is a steep pyramid. Only a tiny few are successful. Only a tiny few make a living at it. The masses do it for love or the tiny chance they will become a star. Almost all of them have day jobs.

- I love it, but with all the commitments I had, I decided to put my creative efforts in another direction. Ones that I had more control of. BTW, I'm available to lecture now because

I'm retired (forgive me; I haven't given you a personal plug in a long time).

- Writing makes me happy. When I was trying to get a lecturing gig at a university, the first question I was asked was: "are you published." I realized that being published would get me more lectures.

- I published my first book "Never Buy a Hat if Your Feet Are Cold—Taking Charge of Your Career and Your Life" in 1990. It was a success. However, the checks I received from the Publisher were only worth a few trips to Vegas.

- I published my second book "The Year of My Death," a novel, in 2003. However, this time was different. I stopped thinking I was going to be a famous author. I followed the two simple rules above. Writing takes a long time. I was willing to give up some of my free time because I enjoyed the writing. It made me happy. The second rule was I wrote it for me. If it didn't sell one copy, that was OK. This was a story I had to get out of my system and I loved every minute of writing it.

- I published my third book "A True Leader Has Presence—The Six Building Blocks To Presence" in 2010. Again I did it for the two simple rules above.

- Blogging makes me real happy. However, writing a book is nothing like writing a blog. A book takes a long, long time. You have to be dedicated to giving that time. A blog takes me a few hours. I can use stuff I've lived. I can use stuff I have a passion for. I get immediate feedback from some of my readers. All of that makes me happy.

Oh, I missed the part when a few years ago I learned to play the guitar. I really suck at it, but rock and roll and country rock fill my heart—that makes me very happy.

I did most of these things while I had a full time job. I found the time to make me happy.

Don't let the future pass you by.
Start today creating your future.
You deserve it!!

BLOG# 26

Valentine's Day—Happy Day?

For many people February 14th is a happy day. For some people February 14th is a not so happy day. The reality is, February 14th is just another day in your life.

The card and gift companies made it an important day. Spacing is critical for their sales. They would never allow Valentine's Day to fall on the same day as Easter, Mother's day, Father's day, Christmas, Chanukah or Thanksgiving.

Sooo, Valentine's Day is just another day unless you want it to be special. I love my wife everyday—not just on Valentine's Day. We do things together all the time—not just on one special day. I love her and she loves me. However, as the blogger who is allowed to speak out of both sides of my mouth, I do get my wife a few Valentine's Day cards.

Two cards from me and one card from my dog Zita. I have to get the card for Zita because she's a lousy card shopper. On Zita's card, she tells my wife how much she loves her (almost as much as she loves food). Zita's speech is limited (duh, she's a dog), so she has to write it down.

Writing it down is important because words on paper (or digital) last forever. Never say something in writing unless you truly mean it. However, with that said, words said or written are today's words—not forever words.

The two cards I get my wife have a purpose. One is a funny card to celebrate my wife's great sense of humor. The other card is a serious card. I look at a hundred cards to find one that has a saying or a poem that represents how I feel about her (hey, I'm a story teller—not a poet).

At the bottom of each card, I write: "you're the best thing that has happened to me" or I "love you today and forever." Even though words are today not forever, words on paper (or digital) last forever. With my wife, I want them to last forever because I will always and forever love her.

Don't make Valentine's Day a special day—make every day a special day to your loved one. Don't send a mixed message on Valentine's Day. A person will take your writings and your gifts as special. They assume you mean what you write. Don't make Valentine's Day a special day unless you truly mean it. Don't make Valentine's Day a special day unless you plan to make the days after special.

For some people, Valentine's Day is not a happy day. It could be because they lost a loved one, never had a loved one, getting rid of a loved one, being dumped by a loved one or just going through a bad time in their life and Valentine's Day reminds them how much their life sucks.

The solution to those people is to remember that February 14th is just another day in your life. If you've lost a loved one, you will get over it and find a new love. If you never had a loved one, think about the other people in your life who either love you or wish you well. Send those people a Valentine's card to tell them you appreciate them in your life. Who knows, maybe next year you'll get a card from them?

If you are (or have) getting rid of a loved one—celebrate. You had the courage to take control of your life and seek a better relationship. If you were dumped by a loved one—celebrate. Better know now than in the future. Moving on is self-healing. Not hating that person is self-healing. You will be with someone who cares for you more than the dirt bag who dumped you on next year's Valentine Day.

Lastly, if Valentine's Day is just a reminder of how bad your life is today, do two things. One, find a mentor who can help you put positive energy back into your life. Two, spend Valentine's Day reading all my blogs. Read and reread them.

They will change your life for the better if you really want it and believe you deserve it.

BLOG# 27

Rainy Day Happiness

It's raining today. In Southern California (SoCal) that's a rarity. When I lived in Philly and New York it rained or snowed most days in the winter and some days in the summer. I now live in Southern California where it rains a few days in the winter and no days in the summer. Because it rains so little, a cold rainy day makes me happy.

When I worked, I loved it when it rained on a Sunday. I could cuddle with my blankie and watch football all day long. I didn't have to walk the dog because it's raining (she has her own pee—pee pad outside). I could turn on my fireplace for the first time in a year. I could stop my hectic life and just veg out. Vegging out a few times a year makes me happy.

Some people feel sad on a rainy day. My son worked in Seattle for a year and had to quit and come back to

SoCal because the rainy and cloudy days made him depressed. I knew he had enough when he sent me an email with the subject: "it just doesn't stop." However, I spent many rainy days in Portland and lived for a year in Amsterdam where I was happy.

In case you don't know, it rains almost all winter in Amsterdam. You see the sun only a very few days. Sooo, how come the Dutch are a happy people?

The answer is simple, when you're happy inside it doesn't matter what the weather is. Some of the nicest and happiest people live in Minnesota where it snows all winter long.

When you live in a bad weather city you realize that everybody is in the same boat with you. You realize that if it makes you happy living in that city (because of family, friends, job, etc.) the weather is not a significant factor to your happiness.

The people who live in SoCal are blessed with great weather. However, in general, SoCal people are not happier than people in Portland, Minnesota, Amsterdam, etc.

One reason is that SoCal people are spoiled. They see the sun so often that when a rainy day happens, they get sad. If they lived in a bad weather city and came to

SoCal, they are so appreciative of the good weather they don't get sad when the weather is bad.

That's my story. I lived many years in Philadelphia. I also spent one year, one month, five days and four hours in Rochester, New York. It rained and snowed all the time. I was unhappy because I had a bad marriage, not because of the weather.

The second reason is the most important. People, who live in SoCal and get sad when the weather is bad, are people who are sad when the sun is out. People, who live in the bad weather in Amsterdam who are sad, are people who are sad when the weather in Amsterdam is great. I could go on, but I believe you get the message.

Positive energy begets positive energy. Negative energy begets negative energy. If you truly believe that saying, then you know the people who get sad during bad weather are the source of negative energy and the people who are happy on a cold rainy day are the source of positive energy.

I'm the latter.
WHICH ONE ARE YOU???

BLOG# 28

Exercise and Happiness

Everybody agrees that exercise is good for your health. What most people don't realize is that exercise is good for your happiness. Some believe that exercise has to happen at a gym. I believe exercise is a goal you set that uses your body or your mind.

By opening up the definition of exercise, you don't have to feel bad because you're not in a gym every day. By opening up the definition you can define exercise as you wish and be proud that you accomplished it. Being proud you accomplished something makes you happy.

Taking a walk on a sunny day is exercise. Reading is exercise. Doing fifty push-ups is exercise. Blogging is exercise. Working out an hour a day is exercise. Cleaning the house is exercise. Vegging out watching mindless TV is not exercising. However, watching something that enhances your knowledge is exercise. These are just a few of my definition of exercise.

The key is in feeling good that you set a goal and you accomplished that goal. It's critical that you like yourself if you want to be a happy and positive energy person. Accomplishing a goal will make you feel good about yourself.

Too many people feel upset with themselves because they don't take the time to exercise. Much of that is because their definition of exercise is working out at a gym. Some of that is because they don't feel good about themselves period. The negative energy inside them enables them to blame everything for their plight.

"I'm not good enough because I don't exercise." "I want to lose weight, but I don't have the time." "I don't believe I have the desire to stay with a routine." "What's the use—I am what I am." Negative—Negative—Negative!

Do you have to exercise to be a positive energy person—NO! Do you have to be thin to be a positive energy person—NO! Do you have to be healthy to be a positive energy person—MAYBE!

Why Maybe? In general, healthy people are happier than unhealthy people. However, your health does not have to define your happiness. I have spinal decease and I'm a happy positive energy person. You can have cancer and still have a positive outlook on life. The more positive you are the better chance you will beat it. The more positive you are the more you will enjoy the life you have left.

Sooo, what am I saying here? Find the time every day to exercise (my definition). Take thirty minutes of your day and walk. Appreciate the things you see while you walk. Every day appreciate the thirty minute goal you set and accomplished it. Do the same with mind exercise. The bigger the goal, the bigger the appreciation. The bigger the appreciation the happier you will be.

Starting out with a huge unrealistic exercise goal doesn't work. You'll probably fail and then feel bad about yourself. You won't have that sense of accomplishment. Start with the lowest exercise goal you're sure you will accomplish. Then, as you feel good about what you accomplished, you can create a higher goal and then a higher goal. More accomplishment—more appreciation—more happiness!

Accomplishment leads to liking yourself. Liking you leads to positive energy. Positive energy leads to happiness. Remember, the goal of my blogs is get people to realize that "Happiness is the Forgotten Ingredient in

Life." There are many things you can do to bring more happiness into your life—exercise is just one of them.

Read and reread my blogs to get other tools that will make you happy.

BLOG# 29

Why Negative Energy Sells

I wish I knew the exact reason negative energy sells. If I did, I would do everything in my power to change it. I have some ideas that I'll share, but they are only my ideas. I would greatly appreciate you writing me to comment on your thoughts.

"Today, at six, NBC Evening News will be covering the train crash that killed forty people, a murder in downtown Los Angeles, the teacher who molested ten students and a dog who was saved in a fire."

Does that sound familiar to you—it does to me. Even the saved dog was in a fire. Negative, negative, negative! Every once in a while the news stations have a heartfelt story at the end of the broadcast. All of one minute in a thirty minute broadcast. The imbalance is ridiculous.

BTW, did you notice that pharmaceutical companies are one of the larger advertisers on the daily news? They even have commercials asking people if they are depressed and if they are, call this 800 number.

Another BTW, I stopped watching negative news a long time ago.

Why do the news stations focus on negative energy? It's simple, it sells. They believe they will get a larger audience with negative news than positive news. Bigger audience—more advertisers—more money! You can't blame the stations for wanting to make a profit. However, I always had hoped that one brave news channel would start a "Good News Network." If I hit the Mega Millions I will start the show. Who knows, it might be a hit and profitable. The fact of the matter is, nobody has tried it so we don't know.

Sooo, if we can't blame the network, who is responsible for all this negative news? It's a simple answer—the people who watch it. If you want to change the balance, stop watching. When I'm mentoring a person who is not happy with his/her life, the first thing I ask that person to do is to take negative energy out of their life. That means, stop watching negative news, stop allowing yourself to be in negative situations and replace your negative energy friends and family with positive energy people.

When a person's life is not going the way they want, negative news has two affects. One, they think that watching some other person's problems will make their problems seem not so bad. This is so not true. I know this because they keep watching the negative news and they're still not happy. If it were true, once they feel better, they wouldn't need to watch it. But, it's not true because they keep watching.

Two, there is a negative person inside all of us. That person was created in the past. It could be from a trauma or family problems that happened when we were young. It could have also been created by loving parents who made us feel not good enough because they wanted to protect us. Simple statements like: "don't cross the street you'll get hurt, don't go near fire you'll get burned, etc., etc." made many of us feel inadequate and not good enough. Feeling not good enough is one of the things that created that negative person inside of us.

For some of us that negative person doesn't control our life. However, for many, that negative person inside of us makes us unhappy. I have that negative person inside me. Over the years and with some mentoring, I've realized what that person is doing to me and have been able to take control from him. One thing that helped was to remove negative news, negative events and negative people from my life.

The main thing I learned about that negative person is he feeds on negative energy. By absorbing negative energy it makes him stronger. It helps him control us. It helps him convince us we're not good enough. It enables him to stop us from making decisions or taking risks that will lead to our happiness. The fact is, the stronger he is the less happy we are.

It's not easy taking control from him. It took me years. The people I mentor usually need six to twelve months before they see what he is doing to them and start making changes to overcome his effect on them. He never goes away, but putting more positive energy into your life will slow him down.

Start today! You have the control to not watch negative news. You have control to avoid and change a negative job. You have control to change or get rid of your negative friends and family. It's not easy. You'll have to make some uncomfortable choices, but if you want to be happy, it's worth the short term pain for the long term gain.

I've said it many times in my blogs and I'm going to say it again:

"NEGATIVE ENERGY BEGETS NEGATIVE ENERGY—POSITIVE ENERGY BEGETS POSITIVE ENERGY."

SCREW THAT NEGATIVE PERSON INSIDE YOU. TAKE CONTROL AND BECOME THE SOURCE OF POSITIVE ENERGY. YOU DESERVE IT!!!!

BLOG# 30

The Light At The End Of The Darkness

Just when I thought life could not get worse, I found myself dealing with an ex-wife who was convincing my oldest boy I was a monster, people who I thought were my friends stopped supporting me and going from having money to living day to day.

Losing a son because I could no longer live a false life with a woman I didn't love, really hurt. He was my first and we had so much in common. We were so close. I was crushed when he rejected me.

Losing friends who I grew up with because they thought I should be miserable for the sake of the children, was a blow I did not expect. I felt so alone. I kept saying to myself: "I'm a good person. Why would they do this to me? I didn't divorce them. I divorced someone they knew was making me so unhappy. Why me God?"

Financially, I had to live with a roommate. Here I am an executive at Xerox Corporation living in a small two room apartment with a sloppy, smelly roommate—UGH!! I had a beat-up old Oldsmobile with less than two thousand dollars to my name—triple UGH!!!

Bottom line, I didn't see any light at the end of the tunnel.

After a few months of "woe is me," I took a step back and thought: "I could stay in this depressed state for the rest of my life or I could think about what I could do to generate a light through all this darkness. Once I put the burden of happiness on my shoulders, things started to turn around.

First, I started to look carefully at the things that were right with my life. I made a difficult decision leaving an unhappy situation. I had to pay the price for that. If I stayed in the marriage, I would have been unhappy, angry and frustrated. I wouldn't have any positive energy to give to my spouse or my kids. I was sure that had I not made this decision, things would have gotten worse, not better. My friends were all wrong. I truly believed this painful decision was for the good of not only me, but for all involved.

Having this strong belief opened a crack of light. I stopped punishing myself and started loving myself. I was able to tell the kids that I was not the best father, but I had forgiven myself. If they decided to have a crappy life so they could blame it on me that was their choice. I was no longer responsible for their happiness.

My youngest boy got the message. He knew what I was dealing with at home and decided to support me. Every hug he gave me opened more light at the end of the darkness. I had to accept that my oldest boy would not come around. However, I allowed myself to be Ok with it because he was protected by his mother (in some ways, too much so).

Then to my surprise, people I knew who weren't considered my "best" friends, came to me and said that although they didn't want to get in the middle of our problems, they would support and care for me through the divorce. What a relief. I felt loved. I no longer felt alone. I appreciated friendship even more. Months and years later many of my so called "best" friends realized how hurt I was and nourished me even more. The light was getting brighter by the day.

Lastly, I decided to leave my roommate and move into a tiny apartment by the beach. The best way I can describe how small the apartment was is when I sat at the end of my single bed to tie my shoes, I hit my head on the wall in front of me. It was small, but it was mine. Although I had to stand up to eat in my so called kitchen, it was my kitchen with my food in it. Apples and peanut butter taste really good when you're happy.

I had a great job. My employees really liked working with me. The other executives respected me. Some became true friends. I was great at my job. I knew I was good enough when it came to work. I knew I would make back all the money I had lost. I was happy with what I had. Any additional benefits that came my way were gravy on a delicious roast.

In a short few months I went from "woe is me" to "I love life again." It happened because

I decided to accept what was happening to me and do my part in creating the bright light at the end of the darkness.

BLOG# 31

Birthday Is Just Another Day

I never liked birthday parties. As a matter of fact I never thought much about my birthday or other people's birthday. I'm sure I got this attitude from my upbringing. We were a struggling working family. Our focus was getting through the day. *Birthday was just another day.*

One year, I saved money and bought my father a birthday card. He thanked me and after reading it, gave it back to me and said: "put this away and give it to me next year." I did the same with my sister. My mom was great and made it clear that no cards or gifts were to be given to her.

Her position was, I love you every day—not just birthday. WOW, that was something that stuck with me then and is still important to me now. I guess I don't focus on my or other people's birthday because I don't want to be hypocritical about it. *Birthday is just another day.*

I can't see me making a big deal about someone's birthday when they are just a casual acquaintance all year round. I can't see me making a big deal about a birthday to a friend who I only see or talk to once or twice a year. I can't see me writing something nice on a card if it's not true. Even if it is true, I'm going to tell them by phone or face to face instead of putting it on a card once a year. *Birthday is just another day.*

I don't even make a big deal about birthday to the people I love and care about because I love and care about them all year round. *Birthday is just another day.*

My wife doesn't buy into this attitude. She loves to send cards to everybody. Hallmark has her picture on their corporate office wall.

I do send cards to my wife because some of them are really funny and I love to see her laugh. I do like having or going to birthday parties because, if they are with people I like, I have a great time. However, that same party could have been on any other day and it would be just as much fun. *Birthday is just another day.*

Many of you want to celebrate the birth day of your friends and loved one. However, all you're doing is reminding that person they're getting old. If you're using birthday to remind someone you care about them, then you're not reminding them all year long. *Birthday is just another day.*

If you're throwing a birthday party because they threw you one, that's a bad reason for a party. Stop the cycle and throw them a party on a day that's not their birthday. If you're sending a card because you're afraid they might think you don't care for them—STOP IT.

Worse, if you believe not getting a card from someone means they don't care for *you*; you must be insecure in your relationship with that person. *Birthday is just another day.*

I'm not saying we shouldn't celebrate birthdays. Shoebox would put a hit out on me. I am saying *birthday is just another day* and should not be used to show your appreciation on that day. Take a conscious effort to show your friends and loved ones your appreciation every day.

Appreciation for them every day will get them to appreciate you every day. That way both of you will realize

Birthday Is Just Another Day.

BLOG# 32

I Love Las Vegas

Las Vegas gets a bad rap. People call it "sin city." Ads say: "what happens in Vegas stays in Vegas." That statement leads to the thought that bad stuff is going on in Vegas. If you go to Vegas you must be cheating on your spouse. This attitude toward Vegas is not true.

I don't belong to the Las Vegas Chamber of Congress or the Las Vegas Community. I'm a transplanted Philly boy who lives and loves in Southern California. However, I've been going to Vegas for over 25 years. Since I've retired, I've been going to Vegas, on average, seven times a year.

Why Vegas? Separating the fact that I live only an hour away (by air) or four hours away (by car) from Vegas, there are many reasons I love Vegas. When I was a business executive my life was meeting after meeting.

My ten to twelve hours a day were scheduled. I was run by the clock on the wall.

There are no clocks in Vegas. None of the hotels display a clock anywhere. Even better, unless you go outside, you have no idea what time of day it is in Vegas. The casinos make sure they tint the few windows so that the gaming, spa, lounges, bars, etc. areas look the same at eight AM and eight PM.

In Vegas I can eat dinner at two in the afternoon or two in the morning. I can get drunk at one in the afternoon or one in the morning. I can just do what I want to do when I want to do it. No scheduling—total control. That makes me very happy.

Vegas is international. If you never get the chance to visit cities around the world or only have been to a few, Vegas has them all. Go to Paris and see the Eiffel Tower. Go to Italy and take a ride in a gondola. Go to Egypt and see the pyramids. Go to New York and enjoy the city. All of this is in walking distance or a short taxi ride around Vegas. I've had the fabulous opportunity to have visited these cities, but seeing them again in Vegas reminds me of the fabulous times I had. That puts a big smile on my face.

Vegas can be inexpensive. You can eat all day for $500 or $19.95. You can see great shows for $300 or $25.

You can get a beautiful room for $500 a night or $19.95 a night.

The way to gamble and not lose your shirt is simple, but hard for some people. Look at gambling as entertainment. When you go on vacation you reserve enough money for airfare, hotel room, food and entertainment. In New York you can't stay at a nice hotel for less than $300-$400 a night. Food is expensive. Entertainment is expensive.

In Vegas, you get to decide. You can stay at a nice hotel for little money and use the difference to gamble. You can eat great for little money and use the difference for gambling. You can spend less on entertainment or don't spend any money at all on entertainment and use that money on gambling.

I make those choices every time I'm in Vegas. Do I want to see a show for $300 or play the penny machines for hours? Do I want to eat a $200 meal or play blackjack? The choice is yours—you're in control. Control makes me happy.

The way I work this out is to reserve, per day, a certain amount of money for hotel, food, entertainment and gambling. The trick is to never spend more than that amount "per day." If I lose that money on gambling on any given day, I go back to the room and watch TV or read or eat a hamburger instead of an expensive dinner.

Never convince yourself you can spend more than your daily allotment today because you think you'll spend less the next day. Don't even think you have a chance to make it up on gambling the next day. They didn't build these fantastic hotels unless they were sure you will eventually lose.

Assuming you're going to win instead of viewing gambling as entertainment, is how people lose more money than they can afford. People that do that don't have fun in Vegas and think its Vegas' fault—it must be because it's sin city.

Remember, you're in control.
You decide your happiness.
Vegas is a way to enhance your happiness if YOU decide to make it so.

BLOG# 33

Compassion and Happiness

My friend Kenny sent me this today:

Dalai Lama (@DalaiLama)

"If we seek happiness for ourselves, we should practice compassion: and if we seek happiness for others, we should also practice compassion."

It's hard to have compassion for someone you dislike—and why should you? It's hard to have compassion for someone you don't know—and why should you? It's hard to have compassion for yourself if you don't think you're good enough—and why should you?

The answer is simple—happiness! Not their happiness—your happiness! When you ask a question: "why should I." I would say: "why not." What's the alternative? The answer is holding a grudge, pissed off, angry, indifference and depression. If you think those alternatives will make you happier—YOU'RE NUTS!!!

Telling someone you feel bad about their situation, is not compassion. Feeling sad inside about what you or others are going through, is not compassion. The reason I say this is because those two things are negative energy. Negative energy does not create compassion.

Compassion is forgiving someone who has done you wrong. Compassion is getting involved in bad things that are happening to people you don't know. For example, feeling sad about people you know or don't know that have cancer is not compassion. Getting involved in doing what you can to rid this world of this horrible disease is compassion.

Forgiving yourself for the mistakes you made, is compassion. Loving yourself just the way you are, is compassion. Loving others just the way they are, is compassion. Giving someone your positive energy is compassion.

How can you have compassion for someone who hates you? It's easy, don't hate them back. If you really want to make them crazy, show them compassion instead of indifference. Throw them compassion instead of throwing a negative energy snow ball back at them.

How can you have compassion for someone who has made your life miserable? It's easy, love them instead of hate them and move on with your life by doing the things that makes you happy.

Please believe me (because I've lived it) loving will help you move on to a happier life faster than holding on to that negative bone for the rest of your life. Have compassion for them and yourself.

Do it for you—you deserve it.

BLOG# 34

There Are So Many Things You Can't Do When You're Dead

"There Are So Many Things You Can't Do When You're Dead"—Mel Brooks in the movie "Life Stinks."

Mel Brooks' movies make me laugh out loud. Woody Allen's movies have the funniest one-liners. Both movies are ones all of us should watch when we're having a bad day. Laughter can change a sad day into a happy day.

The line in the Mel Brooks movie "Life Stinks, "There are so many things you can't do when you're dead," is both funny and serious. In the context of the movie, it's funny. In the context of my blogs on happiness, it's serious.

What are all the things you can't do when you're dead—*everything you want to do right now*? What would you do, right now, if a doctor said you only have three months to live?

Would you:

- Call or see the people you really care about and tell them how much they've made your life better.
- Spend more time appreciating the things you have, the things you see, the things you smell, the things you eat, The love you get, the love you give, the friendships you have, the family you have, etc., etc., etc., etc.
- Take the trip you always wanted to take so you can see the beautiful sights, eat different food, meet new people and enjoy a different culture.
- Stop thinking about the problems of your past. Stop hating the people who have done you harm and pissed you off. Stop being angry and frustrated with yourself.
- Stop worrying about the future because you're going to be dead soon.
- Quit your lousy job and do something that makes you happy even if the money sucks.
- Read that book you always wanted to read. See that show you always wanted to see. Ride a motorcycle. Bungee jump (I think I rather die first).

- Give some of your money to the people you know who need it the most (don't give it all because the doctor *could* be wrong).

That's just some of the things you might do. You should make your own list.

The thing that's so interesting is, you can do all of those things today. You don't need the threat of having only three months to live to get them done. Every one of the actions on the list above is in your control to accomplish right NOW.

We don't do it because we always believe we have time—*a bus coming at you right now might not agree.* We don't do it because it takes effort and we're lazy. We don't do it because some of the things scare us. It's not as scary when you believe you only have three months to live anyway. We don't do it because we don't know how.

Do you think you'll be happier if you take action on your list? You know the answer is YES.

Sooo, let's just do it! Yea, even the bungee jump thing. Here we go—AHHHHHHHHHHHHHHHH.

WOW, we survived.
WOW, we're not going to die.
Hooo-Ray!!

BLOG# 35

What Would You Do If You Won The Lottery?

The chances of anyone winning the lottery are so remote that it's ridiculous to even think about what you would do if it happened. However, your choices do have something to say about whom you are, what you value, what is important in your life and what changes you think will make you happier.

In a capitalistic system money gives you freedom of choice. Most people would use that money to choose the things they believe will make them happier. The point is, are you sure you know what would make you happier? Assuming there are things in your life today that don't make you happy, your belief is the money will change those situations.

Therefore, it is important to take a step back and think about the things in your life that are making you unhappy. If money would solve those problems that would be great, however, most problems in life can't be solved with money. Also, the chances of you hitting the lottery to get the happiness solving money is more than remote—it's no f-ing way.

I truly believe you can solve most of your happiness problems without a money windfall. I did and write my blogs so you can also.

Sooo, assuming you can have a happy life without winning the lottery, then what would you do if you did. It makes me feel good thinking about it so here are the first things I would like to do.

I have a housekeeper who has worked for us for many, many years. She is getting older. She has a bad back. She's had two foot operations. She is very religious and is happy she has the support of the church. I would love to help her stop working and allow her to give all her energy to the things she loves most—her family and the church.

I have friends I grew up with that have been very good to me when I needed them the most. They can live out the rest of their life without my help, but don't have the financial security I would love them to have. I know not having financial problems would make them very happy. Their happiness would make me even happier.

I feel the same about my son, my wife and me. I don't need to buy more stuff, but it would be nice to go to sleep knowing my wife and I are safe from financial disasters. Security is probably the biggest thing most people want. Security in your relationships is something you have some control over. Security in your friendships is something you have some control over. Security in your job is something you have some control over (assuming it's a job you like).

Financial security is something you have some control of if you've been prudent with your money. You have to appreciate and respect money at a young age. If you wait until you're older it may be too late. It's critical to create financial security without praying you're going to hit the lottery.

How much money you need to feel secure is the issue. In my blogs I make it clear you will always have food to eat, air to breath and shelter. Everything else is cosmetic. Spending on stuff you don't need at the expense of feeling financially safe is not happiness. Being addicted to financial security is not happiness because you will never have enough. Preferring financial security is happiness. If you prefer it, then run your life in a way so you will have it. The lottery will not save you.

I don't worry about my financial security because my wife and I planned for it. However, as my father would say: "hitting the lottery wouldn't hurt."

I would love to be able to financially make a difference against the war on cancer. I've lost too many loved ones to that horrible disease. It pisses me off that this country spends billions to go to mars and almost nothing to cure cancer.

Now, don't get me wrong, I like thinking about the things I would do if I had millions. I would love to have a driver so I could go to see my friends at our bar and not worry about drinking too much. My wife and I love to throw parties, but it's expensive and it would be better if we had more space. We do it as often as we can, but dreaming about being able to throw more great parties makes me happy.

I don't need more cars, clothes, jewelry, etc. I'm happier with what I have now than I've ever been before. My focus on hitting the lottery is helping the people I love, financial security for my family and friends, curing cancer, having a driver and throwing more parties. Those are the things that would make me happier than I am right now.

What would you do? Think about it because it might bring out some things in your life you could solve without hitting the lottery.

BLOG# 36

Two Old Jews

It's Wednesday and I'm going to Wolfgangs with my wife and my true friend Kenny. We enjoy Wolfgangs because we love the bartenders, the manager, the food, the friends we know and the new friends we are about to meet. However, the best part of my Wednesdays and Fridays at Wolfgangs is laughing with Kenny.

We consider ourselves two old Jews. The reason is because we *are* two old Jews. We both have that Mel Brooks—Carl Reiner sense of humor. I say something and Kenny says something funny back—ba rump ba bomp bum. He says something and I shoot something funny back—ba rump ba bomp bum.

We laugh about almost anything and everything. Trouble taking a crap at our age is not out of bounds. Having CRS (Can't Remember Shit) makes us laugh. We meet people at the bar all the time, however five minutes after we meet a person, Kenny will say to me: "what was his name." I'll think for a few seconds and say back: "I have no clue." We both get hysterical.

Kenny loves to make shit up. I love calling him on it. He meets a new person and tells her he's a marathon runner. Sometimes, he likes to tell them he's ZEN. I get great pleasure telling the person he's bullshitting them: "please don't believe a thing Kenny says because he loves making shit up." This gets Kenny all worked up. He immediately starts defending himself. "I did run the marathon" (he did, but who knows how long ago—he's old you know).

Then he starts defending his ZENness. Kenny does have ZEN like qualities, but he's far from a person who lives his entire life like a true ZEN person. The fun for me is challenging him when he makes shit up. I get hysterical listening to him defending himself to the person next to him that he only met ten minutes ago.

Kenny loves to be an instigator. He gets great pleasure saying things that gets me in trouble with my wife or someone I meet at the bar. We love making fun at each other in front of other people. We get anybody in listening range to laugh at the both of us.

We embarrass each other. We denigrate each other. We yell at each other while we're laughing at each other.

When it's over, we high five each other and remind ourselves we're just two old Jews.

BLOG# 37

What Are You Doing Today To Enhance Your Happiness

Today is today. Tomorrow is tomorrow. Your mantra should be: "Is what I'm doing today leading me to a happier life." "I'll deal with that tomorrow," is putting your head in the sand. Making today the best day of your life should be your goal.

When you wake up in the morning do you think about what you could do that day to enhance your happiness? Do you wake up in the morning and think about all the negative things that might happen today? If the answer is yes to the former—you get it. If the answer is yes to the latter—read on.

If you think you have some or most control over what's going to happen today—you get it. If you think you have no control over what's going to happen today—you will never be a happy person. The fact is, you do have some or most control of what is going to happen today if you're willing to take the action required to control your day.

Here are just a few examples (please challenge yourself to think of examples that are real to you):

You wake up in the morning and think about your day. "I'm not going to eat breakfast today because I think I'm gaining weight. I have this no fun high stress job I have to spend eight hours enduring. I have no plans tonight so I'll go home, get some take-out, watch some TV and go to bed."

Now, take that same situation and start out your day this way:

"I'm going to eat a small breakfast today because I'm going out to a great lunch with one of my co-workers. I'm gaining a little weight, but I have it under control. I never have and never will let it become a problem. My job is not the best and it does have a lot of stress, but it does pay me a decent wage that I'm using to save for a new car. I've been looking for a better job and I know if I keep looking and speaking to people, something will pop up. I don't have anything going tonight so I'm just going to look forward to pizza. I treat myself to pizza once in a while because it makes me happy. After dinner I can't wait to watch my favorite TV shows."

In both examples it's the same day with the same issues, but one person sees this day as a negative and another sees that day as a positive. It's like the pony story; "two kids go home from school. When they get to the living room, they see a pile of shit in the middle of the floor. One kid says: "Oh no, mom is going to think I put it here and she's going to ground me." The other kid says: "wow, dad bought us a pony." **Which kid are you?**

You have control of your thoughts. You have more control of your actions than you think. You can decide to think of today as a negative or a positive. Positive thoughts will help you become a happier person. Negative thoughts will drag you deeper into the abyss.

Be honest with yourself. Look at the way you see your life. Decide what kind of person you want to be. Nobody who is sane wants to be unhappy. Nobody who is sane wants to have a bad day. Believe it or not, your day can be a happy day if your mind sees the positive in that day instead of the negative.

Don't think you can start doing this any time you want. "I'm going to think positive tomorrow doesn't work." You must start today. It's a brain exercise that must to be reinforced every day. The more you think this way (every day) the easier it becomes.

By doing so, someday you will wake up and see the day as positive without thinking about it. Please start today—you deserve it.

BLOG# 38

What's Love Got To Do With It

In a simple word—*everything*.

Love of life, love of spouse, love of girl/boyfriend, love of friends, love of family, love of job, love of health, love of food, love of animals, Love of weather (I love a good rainy Sunday—some people love snow) and love of blogging (that's me). How many more could you add?

I could change the word love for passion and it would mean the same. It's critical to have love and passion in your life. Your physical and mental health improves when you have love and passion in your life. Your relationship with spouse, friends, family, etc. improves when you have love and passion in your life. Your happiness improves when you have love and passion in your life.

In my opinion it all has to start with a true love and passion for life. Too many of us just go through the motions of life. Some of us just want to get through the day. How many of you wake up in the morning and feel like you're going to have a great day, a great month, a great year and a great life.

Unless people have a serious disorder (like being bipolar or manic), depression comes from not thinking that life is wonderful. Thinking there is a better life beyond this one means this one is not good enough. This is the one you know. The other one is just heresy. How passionate can you be about life if you're counting on a better one after your dead?

What does it mean to have a love and passion for life? It means you want to get the most out of it. You look forward to what life is about to give you every day. You're willing to deal with the difficulties of life because you believe the good stuff will outweigh the bad. You can't wait to try new things. You're willing to take risks that will lead to a better life. You're willing to make changes to create a better life.

Once you have a love and passion for life, you start having a passion for other things that life gives you (new friends, new relationships, new jobs, new challenges, etc.).

What does life mean to you? Are you bogged down by the weight of life or are you lifted up by the opportunities of life? Do you believe that loving life is important to your happiness? If you do then why don't you have a passion for all the things I stated above?

Life is hard. It's easy to give in to the negatives all around you. It takes guts to say: "I'm mad as hell and I'm not going to take it anymore." It takes guts to believe you have the power to create a better life. However, it doesn't take guts to have love and passion in your heart.

Take a step back and think about your life. If you have the love and passion I'm discussing here, you're a happy person. You're someone that others want to hang out with. You're someone that others want to be like. You're someone that wants to give positive energy to the people that have little.

If you're someone that doesn't love nor have a passion for the things I mentioned above, then immediately find the people who do and spend as much time with them as possible.

The more of those love life people who are part of your life, the better chance you have to create the love and passion, I believe, we all want.

BLOG# 39

WAR—What Is It Good For

Today—*Absolutely Nothing*

If you're expecting a left wing blog that war is never necessary—you're wrong. There have been wars that were necessary to preserve the life and freedom we cherish today.

Without the civil war, minorities today would still not have freedom or a voice. The First and Second World War needed fighting to stop evil from taking the entire western world's freedom and forcing us to live like the North Koreans live today.

However, once the atom bomb was developed and unleashed everything changed. It was no longer about men and women fighting other men and women who have different ideologies. It became who could destroy the earth we live on for reasons of ideologies, religious belief, holding on to sacred ground, past wars or other reasons that, I believe, even *they* aren't sure of themselves.

It's not like they want our resources because the only way they can win a war is by blowing up all the resources. It's not like they want slaves because the nuclear fallout will kill off not only the people they're fighting, but themselves. It's not like they want power because there won't be anybody to have power over once we all drop the big one.

It's about saber rattling. It's about, you have a big stick and now I have one also. It's about fear not about future. It's about status not about good living for all.

Does anybody think that any country who threatens the western world's way of life will be allowed to use a nuclear weapon? Does anybody think that a country will risk their existence by using a nuclear bomb on another country? If your answer is yes, you're a person who lives their life in fear and negative energy.

If your answer is no, then why are we in Iraq, Afghanistan, etc. These regional wars make no sense. We're gaining nothing. We're losing a lot. These regions are going to do what they are going to do. We have no control. What are *these* wars good for—absolutely nothing!!

The best way to protect ourselves is the way Israel protects itself. Israel may threaten war, but they're currently not in any war. They don't have troops in countries that don't want them there. They don't have troops fighting someone in a country (like the Taliban) that we're not sure are any better than the powers of the country they are supposedly defending.

What Israel's strategy is to use their resources to infiltrate countries that may do them harm. They use covert operations to protect themselves. Who do *you* think killed the Iranian scientists? Instead of being visible with troops, they use their CIA like resources to stop people from gaining access to their country.

Yes, they have a Homeland Security Agency like ours, but they use more of their resources to know what a potentially threatening group is planning and stopping it from doing harm before they can execute their plan. If we had that kind of security we would have stopped the Twin Towers bombing. If we had that kind of strategy, we wouldn't need to be sending troops into harm's way.

The world is a dangerous place. We need to protect ourselves, but why can't we learn from our mistakes. Did all the dying in Vietnam make our lives better? Did the war in Iraq make us happier? Do we have more positive energy in our life because we're killing and being killed in Afghanistan? If you're answering yes to these questions, please find a positive energy mentor.

War had its place in history, however it no longer does. I can't live my life wanting to fight other people so I can feel safer. I feel safe and will continue to feel safe until I know it's not safe (if that day ever comes). I'm not putting my head in the sand. I just don't want to live a life worrying about something that might happen, but is not happening now.

I see a positive future not a negative future. War is not in my positive future.

BLOG# 40

How To Get What You Want?

Ask For It!

How do you get what you want? Here are a few answers:

- Ask for it
- Take action to get it (in my next blog)
- The reverse (in my next blog)

Ask For It

If it sounds so simple then why isn't it happening? How many of you ask your spouse for sex—very—very few. How many of you ask your boss for a raise—not many. How many of you ask your friends for help—very few. How many of you tell your family what you truly think about their attitude and actions toward you—almost none.

None of us like being told NO. However, too many of us are so insecure about getting a NO, we don't ask. What if you ask your spouse for sex and he or she says not tonight? How does that affect your standing as a human being—it doesn't. You have a better chance of getting sex if you ask for it than if you wait for the other person to initiate it. Many spouses would get excited if the other spouse asked for sex—I know I would.

Do you really believe your spouse, girlfriend, boyfriend or friend with benefits would be mad at you if you asked? If you truly believe that, you're either with the wrong person or you're a wuss. Try it tonight—you really have nothing to lose.

Why not ask your boss for a raise? He or she won't fire you. She won't stop liking you. Most likely he'll respect you for asking. If you've done your homework and can present a good reason why you deserve a raise, the worst response you will get is: "not at this time." "Not at this time" is not a NO! Even if you get a NO, you'll feel good about yourself for asking.

If you don't believe you deserve a raise, don't ask for one. However, look into yourself as to why you don't think you deserve one. If you realize you're not that great at your job, that's being honest with yourself. Don't feel bad your boss isn't giving you a raise. Just do your today job while looking for one where you can excel and deserve a raise.

If you believe you *are* good at your job, but are too insecure to ask for a raise, read my blogs and get a positive energy mentor. Do whatever you can to overcome your insecurity. One way is to just walk into the boss's office, raise your head high and ask for the raise. You might be shocked at the response. Even if it doesn't go as you would like, you'll feel better about yourself for asking.

Asking friends for help is a way to separate the true friends from the acquaintances. Never ask friends for money. Money screws up relationships. However, asking friends for moral support when you're going through a tough time, is something you should consider. If you get a NO or "I don't have time right now," then reevaluate this friendship. Don't refrain from asking for help because you don't want to lose a friend. If you get a NO, this is not the friend you thought you had and it's time to move on. You deserve true friends. Hanging on to the bad ones will not make you happy and won't enable you to get what you want.

Family is a difficult situation. My feelings are that family is just people you're related to—not people who are allowed to make you unhappy because they're family. You need to ask them to stop treating you or other people in your life poorly. They're not so special that you have to put up with their crap. You wouldn't let your friends treat you like that—or would you? If you do, you don't think much about yourself.

Losing a family member who doesn't love you just the way you are, is not like losing a limb. If they don't want to exist in your positive energy—happy world, get rid of them. However, before you let them go, ask them to be a better person toward you and others.

What's the worst that can happen—other family members will be mad at you. If so, let them live with the idiot, but tell them you deserve better.

BLOG# 41

How To Get What You Want Take Action And The Reverse

Take Action

Why are simple things so hard to accomplish? If you want something, you have to go get it. Sounds simple, but too many people can't find a way to get it done.

"I know what to do, but I'm too busy to do it now." "I'll get to it soon." This kind of attitude is for people that don't get what they want. "I know what to do and I'm taking action now to get what I want." "I know if I wait until tomorrow it will never happen." This kind of attitude is from a person who gets what he or she wants.

Too busy to take a night class to learn a trade that makes you happier. Too busy to give your time to do something you enjoy doing. Too busy to write that book that has been burning inside you for years. Too busy to get into an exercise and diet program that will make you love yourself that much more. Do I have to say more—you're NOT too busy. Stop convincing yourself you are.

"I know what to do, but I'm not sure I want to take the risk." "Let me think about it." "I know what to do and there is a risk. I've evaluated the risk and believe if the worst happens, I will recover. I know I won't get what I want if I don't take the risk, so I'm going to go for it. No risk—No reward!"

Which person do you think will get what they want? I think that's a stupid question, but some of you might not. Some of us are so risk adverse that we make ourselves believe we don't need or don't deserve to get what we want. Some of us believe that the risk will ruin our lives which would be worse than getting what we want and deserve. I hope you're not one of those people.

"I know what to do, but I have to make a change to get it." "My life is safe and predictable so why change it—why rock the boat." "I know what to do and I'm going to make the changes necessary to get it." "I've decided I no longer want to stay with this safe and predictable life I've been living." "I'm never going to get what I want if I don't make the changes necessary." "I want more out of life and I'm willing to leave my comfort zone to get all I deserve."

The latter sounds simple, but it's not. Change is scary. Change takes time to get used to. Change has the risk of making things worse. However, living a life that's half full is not acceptable. Believe what you want, but until someone can prove me wrong, this is the only life you are going to get. You won't die if you make a change to get what you want.

Even if things don't go as planned, at least you went for it. At least you won't be living a life of "shouldas and couldas." You'll be proud of yourself and feel positive about yourself. That alone is worth making a change to get what you want.

Bottom line is, you have the power and control to take action to get what you want. Think about what kind of life you want to live. Taking action to get what you want takes guts. Taking action to get what you want takes a strong belief in yourself. Taking action to get what you want will lead you to a better life—a happier life—a more positive life. Isn't that what we all want!!!!

The Reverse

This is an old sales trick to get what you want. Many people don't see themselves as winners. Some think of themselves as losers. Some think of themselves as just average.

People want to be with a winner. People want to buy from a winner. People want to invest with a winner. People want to do what a winner wants them to do. People want to get something they didn't think they could get.

The reverse is a way to get what you want from these people. If a person believes that something is special, they want it. If a person believes only winners will get this thing, they want it even more. This isn't the carrot and stick. This is telling someone they're not qualified to get the carrot so they will want it more.

A person who wants to sell something might say: "I want to sell you this bag, but I have a list of people who will pay more." This old reverse trick has proved time and time again to make the person you're selling to want the bag even more. You close the sale by saying: "OK, I'll sell you the bag at the price you want, but only if you promise you won't tell anyone else what price you paid." The person takes the bag and feels great. The seller got what they wanted in the first place by using the reverse.

"I would love to go on a date with you, but I'm not sure we would hit it off." Right away the person you want to date wants to understand why. That's the first part of the reverse. "Why don't you think we'll hit it off?" "Well you're so great and I probably won't meet your standards." Part two of the reverse. "Thanks for the complement, but I'm sure that's not true. Why don't we go out on a date and find out." "Great, that would make me very happy."

The reverse got him what he wanted. A date with someone he wanted to go out with. I could go on with more examples, but you should think about what you want and how you can use the reverse to get it. Work out the scenario in your head before you approach the subject with the other person. Don't worry if you fail a few times. You'll succeed more times then you will fail.

Getting what you want makes you a happy, proud and positive person. Go for it—you deserve it.

BLOG# 42

A Beautiful Day

I walked the dog this morning and couldn't stop realizing what a beautiful day it is. It's clear, sunny and cool. The trees were flowing in a slow breeze that brushed across my face. The greens and the flowers were vibrant as the natural light of the sun make natures gift a blessing.

Zita only noticed the smell of other dogs on this beautiful landscape, but that's all she needs to make her happy. Every time she stopped to smell, I stopped to appreciate the beauty of my neighborhood. I'm so lucky.

I grew up in the streets of Philadelphia. When there was a day like today, I didn't appreciate it. The neighborhood was not conducive to appreciation. There were no trees or flowers. There were six foot lawns that connected to the sidewalk. Most of the lawns were not groomed. The sidewalk was connected to the blacktop street.

Poles with electric wires hung overhead. No beauty was illuminated from the sun.

Now that I've learned to take a step back and appreciate the wonderful life I have, I feel bad for the people and especially kids who live in the projects. I now realize surroundings have an effect on a person's mental wellbeing. I now realize the negative energy of a neighborhood can affect a person's outlook on life.

My parents never understood this phenomenon. If they had, I'm sure we would have driven to a beautiful scenic place on a great day like today. Even getting a few days of positive energy might have given me a better base to create a happier life. As it was, at 39, I had to figure it out with the help of a Mentor.

Some say, you appreciate life more when you finally get something you never had. I have to agree with that statement because it's my life. However, it would have been nice to not have to overcome so much stuff so late in life. It would have been nice to appreciate nature's beauty on a wonderful day like today when I was much younger.

They say stop and smell the roses. I stopped today. I didn't have any roses, but I did have other beauty all around me—and I really appreciated it.

BLOG# 43

"Yesterday Is History— Tomorrow Is A Mystery—T oday Is A Gift— That's Why We Call It The Present"

Saturday night a friend stated the quote above to me. I looked it up and it was written by Alice Morse Earle. I thought it encompassed the essence of what I have been communicating in my blogs on happiness.

"Yesterday is history" because we don't get to relive it. For good or bad it is what it is so we accept what it was. Being unhappy because it didn't go the way we hoped is frustrating, unhealthy, negative and anti-happy. Focusing on what good happened in our past is happy, rewarding, healthy and positive.

However, my suggestion is, "yesterday is history" so forget about it.

"Tomorrow is a mystery." We don't know anything about the future. We like to think we do, but we don't. Too many of us think the future is negative. Those people are frustrated, unhealthy and unhappy. The ones who see the future as positive are the opposite. However, the fact is the future is a true mystery. To think otherwise is a waste of brain power.

It's good to look forward to the future, but thinking it will be bad or good makes no sense. We're on a journey. The future is not a destination, it *is* the journey. Don't spend time thinking about the future—just enjoy the journey.

"Today is a gift—that's why we call it the present." This says it all to me. Most of us are lucky just to wake up today. The older we get the more we appreciate today. We've been given a present—it's called life. Why make the present we've been given ugly. That really makes no sense.

The present is beautiful if we want it to be. We have a life obligation to make today the best we can. We have the right to see today as a treat not a trick. We have the power to stay away from today's negative energy and focus on the gift of positive energy that's around us.

I love life. I appreciate today. I'm going right now to open my wonderful Present.

BLOG# 44

They Don't Know Shit

Do you seek feedback when you have a product, service or ***life*** idea? Do you seek feedback when you have a strategy, decision or position you want to take? If you do, who do you go to for that feedback?

Friends and family are different than a disinterested third party. Friends and family have to weigh the risk of offending if their honest feedback is negative. The better the friend—the higher their risk. A disinterested third party has no stake in your friendship and therefore can be brutally honest.

Friends and family will first view your idea, strategy, decision or position with a mindset that says what's right about this. A disinterested third party will take the opposite position. They'll look to see what's wrong with what you want to do.

Sooo, which way should you go? One answer is friends and family because you'll get positive feedback that will make you happy. Another suggestion is to go the disinterested third party route because you'll get the most honest feedback even if it means they might call your baby ugly.

The right answer is they don't know shit! You should go to either or both and take in their feedback. All feedback is good, but it's not definitive. Feedback from others is information you should take into consideration, however never do or don't do what they suggest or demand. The reason is because they don't know shit!

You might modify your idea, strategy, decision or position based on their feedback, but only if what they're suggesting makes absolute sense to *you*. The fact is the only way you'll know if you or they are right is to go do it.

If it's a product or service the market will tell you if it's valuable. If it's a strategy—nobody knows if it's good or bad. They may have their own view, but again, they don't know shit! If it's a life strategy, decision or position, you and only you should be making life choices.

The bottom line is, never change what you want to do because they told you to change it. Never hold back from going forward with what you want to do because they think it's a bad idea. Never get caught up in the negative energy of their feedback. The reason I say this is simple:

They Don't Know Shit!!!!!

BLOG# 45

You're Just Making This Shit Up

Don't you just love when people say: "he will never succeed," "I read this is how it's going to happen," "people want this," "I'm sure this is what happened," "You don't have to believe me, just ask them."

Now that I'm much more secure in myself, I have no problem calling people out when they say stuff that's bullshit. My statement to them is "you're just making this shit up.

"He will never succeed." How do they know that? "You're just making this shit up." If he would have said: "in my opinion I doubt he is going to be successful in this endeavor," I wouldn't call him out on that statement. However, when someone makes a definitive statement like "he will NEVER succeed;" they're just making shit up.

"I read this is how it's going to happen." Where did you read that? When did you read that? Who was the person who wrote that? Usually, when you push back on the one who makes those statements, he or she doesn't have any of the answers you asked. When they fumble with the answers, I say to them: "you're just making this shit up."

Probably they read something at some time, but it most likely didn't say definitely "this is HOW it's going to happen." They're just trying to force their opinion on you by making shit up. You have to call them out on it or they'll keep doing it to you and others.

"People want this." What people? Who are these people? When did they say this? Again, you have to ask these questions because you can't let a general statement like that go unchallenged. When they fumble with specifics, tell them: "you're just making this shit up.

"I'm sure this is what happened." How are you SURE? Where did you get the information that made you SURE? Are you just making this up because you want this to happen? If he just would have said: "I'm not sure, but in my opinion, I believe this is what happened." I can live with that statement, but some people feel the need to make bold statements. I say to them: "you're just making this shit up."

"You don't have to believe me, just ask them." Who are THEM? Give me a name. Facts, just give me the facts.

I could go on and on with this, but I assume you get the point. You have to be secure enough within yourself to push back. Don't take their bullshit statements because you don't want to rock the boat. Speak out and call them out. They'll respect you more if you don't just roll over.

When they try to make you believe a definitive statement without proof, say to them: You're Just Making This SHIT Up!

BLOG# 46

What Is Your Life Goal

What is your goal in life? What goal do you have for your children, close friends and loved family members? You should be asking yourself that question every day.

Do you define your life goal as one specific (instead of broad) element? "My life goal is to be rich." "My life goal is to get married and have a great family." "My life goal is to have a great job." "My life goal is to have somebody support me so I can lay back and do nothing." "My life goal is to be popular." "My life goal is to be President." "My life goal is for everyone to love me."

I could go on and on with specific life goals, however "my" life goal is much broader—HAPPINESS.

What is your life goal? Do you think about it or are you going through life taking it as it comes. Do you even care? Can you define happiness? Do you believe: "if I only had "this", I would be happy." Do you know what "this" is? Can you be happy without "this?" How do you know the specific life goals described above will never change as you go through life?

I contend if you believe: "if I only had "this", I would be happy," you'll never get the happiness you deserve. I contend if you don't think about or care about what your goal in life is, you'll not have a fulfilling life. I contend if you're focused on a specific life goal, that goal will change over time. I contend if you don't have a broad life goal, like happiness, you'll miss out on a great life.

Let's say your life goal is to become rich. OK, now you're rich—so what. You'll be able to buy stuff. You'll be financially secure. You'll be able to make decisions that non-rich people can't make. BUT ARE YOU HAPPY???

Let's say your life goal is to get married and have children. OK, that happens and you're happy for now. How do you know that will make you happy for life? Let's say your goal is a great job. OK, now you achieved that goal. Are you sure that after a few years you won't have a different job life goal.

The bottom line is specific life goals will most likely change over time. A life goal like happiness will be with you forever. Wanting that goal for your spouse, close friends, children, loved family members, etc. will last forever.

All of the specific life goals are just individual ways to make you happy. However, they're only one way and most likely they won't last throughout your life. The way that works is to love and respect life. The way that works is to love and respect others all the time. The way that works is to appreciate everything you have, everything others give you, and everything the universe gives you.

The way to be happy throughout your life is "The Three Prescriptions To Happiness," by Ken Keyes Jr. I gave you my interpretation of his prescriptions in a previous blog, but I'll say them again:

* "Ask for what you want, but don't demand it."

* "Accept what's happening for now."

* "Love unconditionally even if you don't get what you want."

Happiness IS the forgotten ingredient in life. Start today to make it your life goal—you deserve it.

BLOG# 47

I Believe I Can Fly

One winner of the TV show "The Voice" performed the song "I Believe I Can Fly." It really got to me because it reminded me of a very down time in my life when I needed to believe I could fly to keep me glued together. I needed to believe I could get through this negative depressing time of my life by truly believing I could control my happiness and take actions to overcome the negative situation I was in. I eventually believed I could fly.

My negative situation was many-many years ago and the song "I Believe I Could Fly" wasn't written yet. The song, at the time, that got me through was "The Rose" by Bette Midler.

I truly believed that in the spring I would become the rose. I was a miserable soul, but had so much love for life that I believed the good times would return. The second paragraph of the song gave me the strength to take the risks and make the tough decisions that were required to make me a happy and a positive energy person again.

I didn't want to be afraid of heartache because I wanted to be the one that learns to love. I didn't want to be afraid of dreaming about a better future because I wanted to be someone who was willing to take a chance. I didn't want to be the one afraid of getting because I wanted to be someone who deserves to get and give. I didn't want to be afraid of dying because I wanted to be the one that loves to live.

Never let life take you down. Always believe life is beautiful and worth living. Never let the negatives in your life make you believe you're not good enough. Always believe you are or will soon become "The Rose." Never let others make you believe you can't do what you need to do to make yourself happy.

Always believe YOU CAN FLY.

BLOG# 48

Word Of The Day—Action

Are you an action person or a stand by and watch person? Are you the one who gets it done or do you wait for someone else to do it? Are you the one who makes the decisions or do you prefer someone else decides? Are you the one who takes responsibility or would you prefer to be the Teflon suit—nothing bad sticks to you?

Are you the one who says "I love you" or do you keep your feelings inside? Are you the one who gets everybody together or are you someone who just joins the group? Are you the one who's full of positive energy or are you the one who absorbs positive energy? Are you the one who's the life of the party or are you the one who stands back and just enjoys the party.

Are you the one who always wants to go out and mingle or are you the one who would prefer to stay home? Are you the one who's looking for love or are you the one who waits for love to come to you?

Interesting questions—eh! Take your time to think about your answers because it's important that you really get to know yourself.

You probably think I want you to be the one who takes action—not necessarily. What I want, what everybody wants, what you want is to be happy. That's the forgotten ingredient in life. Being an action person is great, but not for everyone. Being a "follower" person might not be as much fun, but based on your personality, upbringing, environmental and conditioning; being the action person might not make you happy.

I do believe that action people get more out of life. However, the definition of "getting more out of life" is a personal thing. I'm an action person mainly because I watched my "follower" father get very little out of life. I didn't want to be like him so I did and do push myself into action.

On the other hand, I can't say my father was an unhappy person. Life was hard on him and his family. Therefore, his expectation of what life was available to him was much different than mine. He expected little while I expected a lot. My father had a great sense of humor, told jokes all the time and liked to laugh. In an earlier blog I stated the way I value my life was the number of times I laugh. Based on that definition, my father was a happy person.

My two uncles never did anything interesting. It was rare they went out to dinner, to a movie or a social event. They had little and expected little. However, they were two happy guys. My uncle Harry came over to see us every Sunday. He and I laughed all day long. I hugged him and he hugged me. He made me happy and I made him happy. He was a "follower" person and I was an action person. I was a happy kid and he was a happy uncle.

It's great to be around action people. My wife is an action person. Many times it makes me happy to just follow her. The bottom line is—"be all you can be." That doesn't mean you have to be an "action" or a "follower" person.

It means to love who you are and be happy with who you are.

BLOG# 49

Word Of The Day—Negotiation

Negotiation *is a dialogue between two or more people or parties, intended to reach an understanding, resolve point of difference, or gain advantage in outcome of dialogue, to produce an agreement upon courses of action, to bargain for individual or collective advantage, to craft outcomes to satisfy various interests of two people/parties involved in negotiation process. Negotiation is a process where each party involved in negotiating tries to gain an advantage for themselves by the end of the process. Negotiation is intended to aim at compromise.*

MY TAKE:

"After many years of successful negotiating, I agree with most of the definition above. The part I don't agree with is *"Negotiation is a process where each party involved in negotiating tries to gain an advantage for themselves by the end of the process."* I have found the best result of a negotiation is when both parties end up even. They may not have gotten all they want or they may not have gotten more than the other party, but both parties can live with the outcome."

Most of us view negotiation as something between business people, labor unions and political parties (OH, if only Congress would understand the term negotiation instead of this term—"gridlock"). However, in fact, your life is a negotiation.

While going through life you'll find yourself negotiating with friends, family, spouse, children, YOURSELF and others who, in one way or another, affect your life.

When you discuss with your friends what restaurant to have dinner, you're negotiating. If you don't want to take charge of your life or care about your happiness, you don't negotiate with your friends—you just do what they want to do. If you want to live a life of happiness, you'll ask for what you want and negotiate from there.

If you want something from a friend (love, help, support, acknowledgment, etc.), you're negotiating. Don't expect all your friends to just give you what you want. Don't expect the outside world to just give you what you want—even if you deserve it. Most people put themselves in first position—as they should.

If you want to have happiness in your life, you should always love yourself just a little bit more than anybody or anything else in this world. Therefore, for you and your friend to come out even requires a negotiation.

It's important (but, not mandatory) to be involved and close with family. Each person is as different as fingerprints. We all have different wants and needs. We all have different personalities. For some reason, family members don't see each other as they would see their friends. They see themselves as people who hold the other family members to a higher degree then they do their friends. You may *prefer* your friends to be good to you, but family members *expect* other family members to be good to them.

You may *prefer* your friends to give you what you want, but family members *expect* other family members to give them what they want. Therefore, to be able to be involved with and close with family, you have to become an outstanding negotiator. As you get older you'll realize it's worth the effort.

Do you negotiate with your spouse and children? If not, they or you won't have a happy relationship. Unhappy relationships (friends, family, spouse and children) lead to an unhappy life. If you want to have a happy relationship with your spouse and children, you have to be willing to negotiate.

Remember, for *your* happiness, both parties need to come out even. Tell them what you want, but be willing to negotiate the details. Expect them to give up something they want, but be willing to bend on some of the things they believe are "show-stoppers." You want to have all the happiness you can get in your life. The way to get it is to have a happy relationship with your spouse and children.

The easiest one to understand is negotiating with "others that in one way or another affect your life (your contractor, your boss, your plumber, etc., etc. etc.). The only point I will make to you is negotiate to "even" for both parties. Don't hold on to the bone until you get what you want. Don't try to feel superior because you got them to cave. Don't go away from the negotiation knowing they're really unhappy with what they got out of the deal. Please believe me you will lose in the long run—"what goes around—comes around."

It is not worth the stress to fight for every penny. To make yourself unhappy just so you can say you won is just not worth it. It is not worth your happiness to know *they* wound up unhappy. Happiness begets happiness—unhappiness begets unhappiness. Be the source of happiness.

Lastly, you should be conscious of the negotiations that go on inside yourself. Yes, you do negotiate with yourself. Should I take this job, How much money should I ask for, should I tell my spouse I'm not happy with our relationship, should I try tough love with my son, who should I go to solve this problem are some of things you negotiate with yourself. The point is that having that negotiation with yourself is healthy. The more you're in tune with yourself the better.

The goal is to end the negotiation with yourself knowing you can live with the outcome. Ignoring the negotiation with yourself and just letting someone else make the decision will suck the happiness right out of you.

The bottom line is happiness *is* the forgotten ingredient in life. The real goal of any negotiation is leaving with your happiness intact or enhanced. Repeat this statement over and over again.

"IS WHAT I'M DOING OR ABOUT TO DO, LEADING TO MY HAPPINESS!!!"

BLOG# 50

Word Of The Day—Patience

Maybe you've heard of the old joke: "two vultures are sitting on a high mound in the desert looking at a person dying of thirst and exposure. One vulture says to the other: "patience hell, I'm going to kill that sucker."

Patience when it comes to your happiness is a double edged sword. If you're too patient life will pass you by. If you have no patience at all, the stress will leave you unhappy. Therefore, where is the balance? Are you in balance? Do you know yourself well enough to evaluate your patience level? Do you know situations well enough to know when to be patient and when not to be patient?

As you can see, I'm putting the patience meter on YOU! I know my patience meter. I know my patience balance. I know the answer to the questions above—do YOU?

Happiness is the forgotten ingredient in life. Patience plays a significant role in your happiness.

They say patience comes with age. For me, that statement is true. I didn't have any patience before 30. It affected my happiness in both my business and personal life. 40 is when I started to understand that being impatient was not making me happy. At 30, I had little or no patience with my kids, my wife, car drivers, stupid people, incompetent service people, my bosses and my employees. My impatience not only stressed me out, it also stressed out the people I was dealing with. This made all of us unhappy.

Around 40, I started to realize the outside world will not always act or do what I wanted them to do. Stupid people don't want to be stupid—it's just their DNA. Hiring incompetent people is my fault. Hire someone else. Car drivers just don't care about other car drivers so what's the sense in being impatient with them.

Kids are just that—kids. Their impatience meter is off the chart. Therefore, the more patient I became with them, the more patient they became. The same is true with your spouse.

Being impatient with my bosses didn't work. I realized I had two choices. One, accept that these bosses were not going to move at my pace and find ways to encourage them to move faster. Two, realize I can't live with their pace and knowing it will not change, move on to a different job that has different bosses or find another company that might have better bosses.

In my long career I did both. I took different jobs within the company to work for people who were on par with my patient meter. Some of these jobs were deemed a demotion by others. I saw them as a happier work environment which led to getting more done and getting promotions. I left Xerox to go to a smaller more aggressive technical company because I could not live with the pace of Xerox's upper management. I gave up a lot of money and security, but I gained a lot more happiness.

You may say: "why do I have to be patient? Why can't they stop treating me like this? The answer is simple—happiness. Not my happiness—not their happiness—YOUR HAPPINESS!!

Before you react, take a deep breath and consider if your impatience will lead to your happiness. Impulsive reaction to situations or people usually leads to overreaction—which usually leads to impatience—which usually leads to unhappiness.

Now, because I'm the one writing this blog, I get to talk out of both sides of my mouth. The other side of the "patience's" double edge sword is being too patient. I would not have achieved senior level positions in business if I was too patient. I would not have been able to get the most out of my employees if I was too patient. I would have never left my first wife if I was too patient. Being too patient would have led to years of unhappiness.

The bottom line is to understand your patient meter. Try to get your patience/impatience in balance. Not too much—not too little—just right. Lastly, focus on your happiness. Be patient if it makes you happy. Be impatient if it makes you happy. Don't be patient if it makes you unhappy. Don't be impatient if it makes you unhappy.

Happiness is your goal because
YOU DESERVE IT!!!

BLOG# 51

Word Of The Day—Frustration

One of the definitions of frustration is: "*a deep chronic sense or state of insecurity and dissatisfaction arising from unresolved problems or unfulfilled needs.*"

I found it interesting that Webster relates frustration to insecurity. After much thought, I can understand it on some level. What I'm sure of is frustration leads to anger and anger leads to unhappiness. Therefore, I was going to make this blog about why you should take frustration out of your life. Simply said: "less frustration—more happiness. More frustration—less happiness".

What I didn't plan on writing about was why some people get frustrated. People who are happy in life don't expect the outside world to make them happy. People who are unhappy in life are only happy when the outside world gives them what they want. However, much of the reason some people live via the outside world is because they're insecure.

When I first went to my mentor, he asked me: "why are you seeing me." My answer was: "well, if everybody would stop treating me like this, I wouldn't need to see you." It took me a year to understand why that statement was supporting my frustration with life and making me unhappy.

If you get frustrated when your friends, spouse, family members, boss, co-workers, etc., etc. do things that frustrate you, think about why you're getting frustrated. You don't want to get frustrated. You know that being frustrated doesn't make you happy. Sooo, why not just stop getting frustrated?

The answer could be the root of your frustration in the first place. Nobody wants to admit they're insecure. They believe if they're insecure there is something wrong with them. They believe if they're insecure they're not good enough. The facts are all of us are insecure to some degree. To some degree our parents were insecure when we were young and they passed it down to us (as their parents passed it down to them).

When someone says to you: "you're insecure," do you get a pain in your gut? If you do it's because you *are* insecure. Do you try to defend yourself if they say: you're insecure? The more you defend the more insecure you are. The more experience you get the more confidence you get. The more confidence you get the more secure you get. Don't hate your insecurity because the more you resist the more your insecurity will insist. Accept the level of insecurity you have and know you'll be more secure in the future.

Insecurity makes it hard to stop getting frustrated. People who have no patience get more frustrated than people who have more patience. Maybe people who have less patience are more insecure. I'm not sure, but when I was young, I had little patience and was frustrated a lot. Now, I'm much more patient and get frustrated a lot less. I'm also much more secure within myself than I was when I was younger.

I get more frustrated with myself because I know I can do better. I get much less frustrated with the outside world because I don't count on them making me happy and I now know I'll recover from anything they throw at me. My security and confidence in myself has led to a happier life. After reading the definition of frustration for the first time, I'm a believer that my security and confidence in myself has made me less frustrated in life.

My previous blog(s) deal with insecurity and the effect it has on your happiness. Please reread them because if you can fix some of your insecurities you will probably be less frustrated.

Less frustrated—more happiness.
More happiness—less frustrated.
The circle goes on and on!!!

BLOG# 52

Relationships

I've been through many relationships (three wives, girlfriends, friends and family). Each relationship is like fingerprints—all different. The one thing I believe is critical is that relationships are critical to life. Good relationships make you happy. Bad relationships should create a learning experience so you won't make the same mistake twice. If you take a positive attitude toward a bad relationship, you can appreciate the experience and turn a negative into a positive.

Good relationships take effort on your part. Expecting the other person to make the relationship work just doesn't work over the long haul. The best relationships are ones where both parties give at least half. The best relationships are ones where both parties communicate their hopes, dreams, loves, happiness and sadness to each other. The best relationships are ones where both parties root for the other party to succeed and find happiness.

The best relationships are ones where both parties support and protect each other from the negative outside world. The best relationships are ones where both parties accept the quirks of the other party and love them just the way they are. The best relationships are ones where both parties don't expect the other party to run their life. The best relationships are ones where both parties don't make loans to the other party. The best relationships are ones where both parties find a way to have fun with each other.

If you're in a one-way relationship, eventually you'll resent it and when the slightest problem occurs, the relationship will start to fall apart. If you're in a one-way relationship and the dominate party disappoints the other, the relationship starts to fall apart. If you're in a one-way relationship you lose your identity—no identity—no happiness. If you're in a one-way relationship it's hard to be heard—no voice—no happiness.

The bottom line, one-way relationships just don't work over time. Some people take a long time to figure it out. They don't want the relationship to end so they make themselves believe that things will change. Some people figure it out and realize it will never change, but they stay in the relationship because they have no confidence they will find a better one. Those people will never be happy positive energy people.

I was in such a relationship with a friend when my true friend Kenny (yes the other Kenny) said to me: "Kenny, you have to divorce this friend." I never thought of it as a divorce, but he was and is right. I divorced two of my wives because the relationships stopped meeting the criteria of the "best relationships" stated above. However, I never thought that ending a relationship with a friend or family member was a divorce. The fact is, Kenny is right. It's a divorce and has all the heartache and headache of a divorce.

The goal of any relationship should be to try to make it work. Good relationships are good for your soul and your happiness. If the other party makes a mistake (even if it's a big one), don't give up on the relationship because you're angry. Anger is negative energy and will only bring more negative energy to the relationship.

You can be the one to forgive and forget. Forgiving and forgetting is positive energy and will make you a happy person. Obviously, if the other party continues to screw up, the relationship is over. However, if you can end it without anger and frustration, you're the big winner. Ending a relationship with anger and frustration doesn't serve you and your happiness. Always remember:

HAPPINESS IS THE FORGOTTEN INGREDIENT IN LIFE.

IS WHAT I'M DOING OR ABOUT TO DO LEADING ME TO MY HAPPINESS?

IF NOT DO SOMETHING ELSE—LIKE FORGIVING AND FORGETTING!!!

BLOG# 53

Why Do You Contribute

Why do you contribute? What do you contribute? To whom do you contribute? What's it my business?

Actually it's none of my business. Contribution is a personal thing. However, taking *me* out of the equation, it should be important to you to understand why you contribute, what you contribute and to whom you contribute. It is important because contribution should have a role in your happiness.

A guilt contribution will never make you happy. An ego contribution will never make you happy. A tit for tat contribution will never make you happy. Contributing because you believe it will wash away your sins will never make you happy. A tax deduction contribution will never make you happy. Contributing because you truly care for a cause will make you happy. Contributing because you believe your time or money will make a difference will make you happy. Contributing because you want to build something will make you happy.

Many years ago I was in my house of worship on the High Holidays. This was a time to think about your life and how you could become a better person. After the service was over, the head religious guy starts reading, out loud, the contributions the people in the audience gave. "The X family gives $500." "The Y family gives $1000." "Mister A gives $1500." "Mrs. Z gives $2000."

I was disgusted! I was there for self-introspection. I'm not a religious person, but I felt a place of worship was a good place to think about my life. However, the X and Y family were there to have everybody applaud their contribution. The A and Z people were there to show off their contribution to the other people. They didn't care about the High Holidays. They didn't care about the house of worship. All they cared about was their ego. I'm sure they were depressed when they heard that someone else gave more than them.

Did you ever have someone tell you: "I have to give at least this amount because Mary is giving this amount. Does that meet my reasons for contributing—I don't think so. Did someone ever say to you: "I give to my charity because I need the tax deduction." Does that contribution have anything to do with that person's happiness—NO! Did someone ever say to you: "I go to church every week and put money into the box so I'll be forgiven for my sins." Does that person even care about the church and what it stands for—I don't think so!

What do you contribute? It depends on what is more valuable to you. If you're contributing for the right reasons, your contribution should be something you value. If you are a millionaire, giving $1000 to a cause is better than nothing, but it could mean you don't care about the cause. The millionaire's time has more value to her or him. Giving that time to the cause probably will bring more happiness because they're involved in the cause.

Giving more than you can afford will not make you happy. When you give more than you can afford, it will take away from other things in your life. It's good to be involved and give to a cause, charity, etc. but, don't ever give more than you can afford because you'll resent the cause when it starts taking away the time or money you want to use for other things that make you happy. In my experience, people who give more than they can afford do it out of guilt or ego. Doing anything out of guilt or ego will never make you a happy person.

To whom do you contribute? You have a valuable asset. It could be your time or your money or both. Those assets should be used for your happiness. That's not being selfish because the happier you are the more positive energy you have to give. The more positive energy you give the more positive energy you get back. The circle goes on and on.

I know you were not brought up that way—I wasn't. I know it doesn't sound right, but giving more than you can afford just doesn't work. What I found out was giving more than I was getting was not making me happy. When I was not happy, the people around me didn't benefit. When I was getting at least as much as I was giving I was happy and the people around me were happier. If you want to be the source of positive energy never give more than you get back.

Make sure you focus all of your contributions on organizations or people you truly care about. Make sure you focus all of your contributions on things that will lead to your happiness. You deserve it.

BLOG# 54

When Was The Last Time You Cried

Crying, like laughing, is an endorphin release. It releases stress. It can make you feel a huge burden has been lifted off your shoulders. It can put a smile on your face. Five minutes after, you could feel fantastic. You can get sympathy from others. It can make you look weak. It can make you look emotional. It can make you look out of control. It can screw with your macho facade. It can make others cry. You can lose a job opportunity. You could get the job. Others might think you're a cry baby.

Sooo, is crying a good thing or a bad thing? I'm going with a good thing. However, many of you think it's a bad thing and do everything you can to not cry. It's not just men. Many women have the same problem in this women's lib era. Trying not to cry is not natural. You're stopping the body from doing what it wants to do. It's like trying not to go to the bathroom when you have to pee or poop. We all know that doesn't end well.

Crying can depend on why your body wants to do it in the first place. If you're watching a movie that's so funny you start crying, don't try to stop it. It's a reaction to the flood of endorphins that are being released from your frontal lobe. Holding back could make a negative out of a positive. If you just experienced a tragedy, crying is necessary because if you don't, you'll get even more depressed.

If you're crying because you lost a tough game, that just means you're very competitive. If you're crying because you won a tough game, that's you being really happy. If you're crying because you lost an earring, let it out and immediately remember it's just a thing that can be replaced. If you're crying because you lost your wallet, let it out, but remember crying won't get it back. You just have to go through the trouble of replacing everything. If you're crying because someone has more than you, that means you don't get it and have to go back and read all my blogs.

If you're crying because you're depressed, let it out and don't force a stop. Accept what's happening for now and get help. Avoiding depression is very bad. It may be personal, physiological, chemical or all of the above. The worst thing you can do is to try not to be depressed and try not to cry.

If you're crying because you can't get what you want—get a life.

Focus on what you do have, not what you don't. After the cry is over, find something to laugh about. Always remember, you're in control of your happiness. You can choose to be a happy positive energy person or an unhappy negative energy person. Which one do you think is better?

I love crying over a great laugh. I cry every time I see the ending of the movie "Sleepless in Seattle." I cry when I see others suffer. Am I emotional? I hope so. Showing my emotions is letting my body do what it wants to do. The people I care about love me even more because I can show my feelings.

Do I look less macho? Who cares! What's it their business? I don't even know what it means to be macho and I don't care. I know they love me just the way I am. Do I look out of control? Everybody who truly knows me knows I'm in charge of my life and my happiness—are you?

Do I use crying to get sympathy from others—never? Using crying as a tool might be good if you want a part in a movie, but forcing your body to cry for sympathy reasons is manipulation. The body doesn't want to cry. Therefore, you're forcing the body to do something it doesn't want to do. That's not a good thing and will not make you a happy person (unless acting is the job you always wanted).

You're never a cry baby if you cry because you need to. You are a cry baby if you're forcing it to get your way. Cry babies are negative energy people. Showing your emotions via crying is positive energy. If it's real, others might cry along with you. If they do, it must be striking a nerve inside them. That nerve needs the release of crying. Hugging while the two of you are crying can create a bond that could last forever.

We all have buttons inside of us that when pressed tells the body to cry. Putting up barriers to prevent your buttons from being pressed will not lead you to happiness. Go watch a movie that presses a button and get a good cry. You'll feel fantastic five minutes afterward. Don't try to cry, just let the body do what it wants to do. You'll be a happier person for it.

I don't cry often, but when it happens, I know it's for the best. I know I'll be happier if I let it out. I know my true friends will understand and stand by me. I know if it's for happy or sad I will get something positive out of it.

BLOG# 55

Pain

There are three kinds of pain—physical, mental and pain in the ass. Forget about pain in the ass because we all know those are the people we should avoid.

Physical pain is different than mental pain; however, believe me, both hurt the same. Physical pain can be taken care of with physical treatment, operations, drugs, talking to a therapist/mentor or all of the above. Mental pain needs time, positive support from friends and family, drugs, talking to a therapist/mentor or all of the above.

Chronic physical pain is pain that won't be healed by treatment or operations and might kill any chance you have at happiness. Drugs can get you through the day, but we all know the downside of being addicted to drugs. Talking to a therapist/mentor can help a lot if you're willing to accept your pain.

I have chronic pain. I've had a four level bone/disk fusion surgery in my neck because I lost the use of my left arm. My arm is much better, but some of the pain and numbness is still there. I have Spinal Stenosis. This is an arthritic condition in my lower back that causes pain and numbness down my legs. An operation is not recommended because the risk of permanent damage is high.

WOW, is this blog a downer. Not really. As I've told you in previous blogs, these are the happiest years of my life. How could that be? It's not easy, but I have accepted my chronic pain. It's part of who I am. I have two choices. Be miserable all the time and blame the outside world (and my father—he had the same condition) or accept what's happening and focus on the positive energy in my life.

The people who love me feel bad because I have this pain. My response to them is: "I'm OK. It's just the bumpers. My engine and transmission are in great shape." I have accepted my lousy bumpers.

I rarely talk about my pain because talking about it makes me focus on it. Instead I focus my energy on the things I love. I focus on the things that bring me positive energy. I focus on the things that make me happy. The love of my life, my wife, makes me happy. Blogging makes me happy. My dog Zita makes me happy. Playing my guitar makes me happy. My good friends make me happy. The people I mentor make me happy. Exercising makes me happy and, oh yes, Jerry Springer makes me happy—Jerry, Jerry, Jerry!!

I've also had mental pain. Two divorces, my oldest son not talking to me, losing close friends who were angry with me because of my first divorce and losing all my money twice is a lot of mental pain.

The things that helped me through my mental pain and depression were, time to heal, a year and a half with my therapist/mentor, friends I didn't expect who supported me when I needed them the most, losing my anger, accepting what was happening for now, asking for what I wanted, but not demanding it, loving unconditionally even if I didn't get what I wanted and truly believing better days were coming.

Seeing the future as a positive can be a cure for all that pains you. Believing life is worth living and living it to the fullest can be a cure for all that pains you. Focusing on what you have not what you don't have can be a cure for all that pains you. Being around people who love and respect you can be a cure for all that pains you. Giving positive energy out to the universe can be a cure for all that pains you.

Caring for and being there for the people who are in pain can be a cure for all that pains them. Helping them get through their pain will make you happy.

BLOG# 56

Listen To The Music

What's your favorite song? I have many. Some bring back good times and some bring back difficult times. A favorite song shouldn't be one that sounds great or has a great beat. A favorite song should be one that stirs an emotion deep inside you. A favorite song should be one that brings back a strong memory. A favorite song should be one that states your feelings for someone else. A favorite song should be one that when you're sad, hearing it played makes you happy.

One of my favorite songs is "The Rose" by Bette Midler. It brings back strong emotions of a time when I was at my lowest point. It gave me hope that the future would be brighter. I could be that "rose" in the song. Once I started believing in my future, I had the strength to take the actions necessary to make a better life for myself. I took those actions because I listened to the words and the music of "The Rose."

Other favorite songs of mine are music from the 50's. When I hear the Spinners, Temptations, Four Tops, The Cadillacs, The Coasters, The Delfonics, The Del-Vikings, The Flamingos, Frankie Lymon, Kool & The Gang, Lloyd Price, The O'Jays, Otis Redding, The Platters, Sam & Dave and Wilson Pickett, they all bring back a time in my life when things were simpler, less stressful and a whole lot of fun.

"At 10, I was poor, but I didn't know it—I was having fun." That's a line in my first book "Never Buy A Hat If Your Feet Are Cold—Taking Charge Of Your Career And Your Life." Everybody in my neighborhood was in the same financial boat. We grew up together, played together, laughed together and when we were 16, sang together until I was 19. The songs we sang were from the artists listed above. When I listen to those songs now, they remind me of those good times.

I love the song, "You Are So Beautiful" by Joe Cocker. It's a simple song and the one I gave to my wife:

"You are so beautiful to me—you are so beautiful to me—you're everything I hope for—you're everything I need—you are so beautiful to me."

Years after I met Ellen we were in Japan on business. Our guests took us to a karaoke bar after our meetings. Everyone was singing songs from the music box. I decided to sing "You Are So Beautiful" to Ellen a cappella. It was a big hit with my hosts and I could see the love in Ellen's eyes—that made me very happy. Finding a simple song with limited words with or without background music can make you happy. Sooo, what's stopping you?

The brain retains music and pictures better than words, numbers or events. The brain doesn't remember physical pain. It knows you had pain, but you can't *feel* that pain after it's over. Think about a time when you were in physical pain and got over it. You can talk about that pain to others, but you don't "feel" that pain again. The same thing is true about times when you were happy and laughing. You can tell people about the good times, but you don't relive them physically.

However, when you hear music or see a picture of a time when you were happy and laughing you can physically have a smile on your face and laugh again. Make music part of your life. Every day, play the music that made and makes you happy. Music can bring you positive energy. Positive energy brings you happiness.

Music—happiness—positive energy—more happiness—more positive energy—more music.

BLOG# 57

Anger

Anger is *"an emotion related to one's psychological interpretation of having been offended, wronged or denied and a tendency to undo that by retaliation. DeFoore, describes anger as a pressure cooker; we can only apply pressure against our anger for a certain amount of time until it explodes. Anger may have physical correlates such as increased heart rate, blood pressure, and high levels of adrenaline and noradrenaline. Anger is part of the fight or flight response. Anger can have many physical and mental consequences."*

"The external expression of anger can be found in facial expressions, physiological responses, and at times in public acts of aggression. While most of those who experience anger explain its arousal as a result of "what has happened to them," psychologists point out that an angry person can very well be mistaken because anger causes a loss in self-monitoring capacity and objective observably. Modern

psychologists, in contrast to the earlier writers, have also pointed out the possible harmful effects of suppression of anger. Displays of anger can be used as a manipulation strategy for social influence."

OK, so now we know what anger is, why we have it and how we display it. Therefore, I guess it's OK to get angry—not always. Anger has its downside. Anger screws up your chi. Being angry brings you negative energy. Being angry affects your mental and physical health. Being angry can make others angry. Being angry doesn't make you happy.

Sooo, why get angry? Many of us don't have a choice. Someone hits your car—you get angry. Getting angry won't fix your car nor will it change the person who hit your car. What getting angry will do is upset you, depress you, slow you down from taking action needed to get the car fixed, make the other person react defensively instead of feeling sorry for what he has done and affect you physically.

You shouldn't try to stop getting angry when someone does something bad to you, but you need to get over it quickly. Not for them—get over it for YOU. Staying angry over a single situation for a long time doesn't serve you or your happiness. Remember, "is what you're doing or about to do making you happy.

What should be your "I'm in control of my happiness" response when someone does something to piss you off? Get angry then take ten deep breaths and focus on what you have to do to fix what made you angry in the first place. In the car situation, after your ten deep breaths, get the person's information, take pictures, call the police and focus on how you're going to FIX YOUR CAR! Getting angry won't fix it—you have to get it fixed.

If you're really enlightened and only care about your happiness, consider that the other person who made you angry didn't do it on purpose. Maybe he or she is not a bad person. Maybe he or she feels bad about what they did. Maybe they had something bad happen to them that day and they didn't pay attention to what they were doing. Maybe they're unhappy people filled with negative energy and hate themselves for what they did.

The bottom line is, being angry with them will not make you happier. Believe it or not (I believe because it has changed my life), caring about them "will" make you happier. If you really want to be a happy person, be the one who cares not the one who hates. Then GET YOU CAR FIXED!

Sooo, why do we really get angry? The answer is when someone or something does something bad to you it presses a button inside you. We all have these buttons.

These are negative energy buttons. "You should have done this," presses the "I know I should have done that and I'm angry with myself" button. "I hate your attitude," presses your "I'm not good enough" button. This button usually makes you angry with yourself and the person who pressed that button. You get defensive and show your anger to the other person to protect yourself. Finding out someone cheated on you presses your "I'm not worthy button." This makes you angry and depressed with yourself and you take it out on the cheater.

The answer to why we get angry is to get rid of your buttons. The wrong answer is to be angry with the people or events who are pressing your buttons. This is very hard to do. Some of my blogs can help. Loving yourself, being confident in yourself, accepting yourself just the way you are, knowing you're a good person who does the right things and accepting that the outside world will always find a way to press your buttons, but you choose not to react, ***is your mantra***.

Happiness is the forgotten ingredient in life. You can choose to not allow anger to take you down. You can choose to limit the amount of time you stay angry. You can choose to accept (maybe even love) the people or events that are making you angry. You can choose to love life more than you love being angry. You can choose to get the help necessary to minimize the affect your buttons have on you.

ANGER, WHAT IS IT GOOD FOR— ABSOLUTELY NOTHING!!!

BLOG# 58

Weather Affects Emotions

A little known fact is the suicide rate in Southern California goes up when it's rainy or cloudy for two weeks or more. Another fact is the suicide rate in Minnesota and Rochester, New York is lower than Southern California and does not go up during the horrible winter weather.

I spent one year, one month, five days and four hours in Rochester, New York. Needless to say, I was extremely happy when I was promoted to a job in Philadelphia. After living in Rochester, Philadelphia seemed like Florida. I started thinking about why weather can affect your emotions. Why are people in Minnesota and Rochester more acclimated to lousy weather than other cities? Could the old joke be true?

"A friend asks his buddy: "why do you let your wife hit you over the head every day?" The buddy responds: "because it feels so good when she stops."

I know in the times I've spent in Philadelphia, Portland (it rains almost all the time) and Rochester, New York that when the rain, snow or clouds stop, it feels so good. People in Minnesota, Rochester, Philadelphia and Portland buy convertible cars. What are they thinking? The weather sucks, but when it gets better (even a little better) they leave their houses or even work, get in their cars, put down the top and ride baby ride.

After much thought, I don't think it's because of the old joke. I think it's rooted inside people's emotions. My son spent a year in Seattle. At the time he was a surfer boy from Orange County, California. He left for a better job. About six months into his new job, I got an email from him with the subject: "It just doesn't stop." It was the clouds and the rain that were getting to him. He started to get depressed. After a year he, with my blessing, left his good job and the stock options he had accumulated to come back to Southern California.

As it turns out, the weather was not his problem (although he blamed it on the weather). His problem was he expected the job to make him happy and it didn't. He thought seeing the sun, the beach and the waves would make him happy—it didn't. It wasn't easy, but thirteen years later, he began to love, trust and have confidence in himself. He realized he had accomplished a lot in his life and was a good person. Most of all, he believed he was good enough.

As he became more mature he realized and appreciated his life and the places where he had been. Seattle is a beautiful and great city. Today, he's married to a fabulous wife, has two kids and is a lawyer. He has no problem with the weather no matter what city he visits.

If bad weather is making you blue, look inside at what's really going on. If you need good weather to make you happy, look inside at what's really going on. You can't count on the outside world to make you happy. The weather is the outside world.

There is nothing wrong with appreciating a beautiful day. Appreciating anything and everything in life will make you happy. However, that beautiful day is a bonus (not a need) to your happiness. Get all the bonuses you can get just don't demand them to be happy.

Rochester and Portland got me to appreciate where I live in California. I wouldn't want to live anywhere else. However, I had fun in Portland. I have a true friend in Portland. I have family I love in Portland. I've had and have eaten great food in Portland. And, OH—YES, it feels so good when the rain stops.

I hated the weather in Rochester, but I made great friends. We were all in the same boat. Instead of going out all the time, we spent time together in each of our houses having parties. The weather actually did a good thing—it brought us together. The bad weather was expected and therefore, was not the focus of the people who were going to live there the rest of their lives. If they weren't happy it wasn't because of the weather and they knew it. I wasn't happy in Rochester because I had a bad marriage, not bad weather.

Happiness is the forgotten ingredient in life. Happiness is your goal. A good weather day should be a plus to your happiness. A bad weather day will bring up emotions that you need to get in tune with. Once you're in control of your emotions, once you're focused on positive emotions instead of negative emotions, the weather will not rule your happiness.

PS. It's cloudy today and has been for three days, but I'm still having fun.

BLOG# 59

Just Ask The Lonely

During my first divorce I felt like the loneliest person in the world. My wife hated me. My oldest son hated me. My best friends were cold to me. I lived almost an hour away from my kids. I was new in LA and didn't have any friends—I just had a few business acquaintances.

I felt really lonely. Three things kept me glued together. I was really good at my job and was respected by my employees and my management. My job was my salvation because, at the time, I needed it to help me feel good enough. I believed everybody else thought I was a loser.

I met a woman who believed in me. Juanita and I tried to have a sexual relationship, but when that didn't work, she stayed my friend. She and I were really close and did many things together. She loved me just the way I was (which was all screwed up) and that made me feel less lonely.

A friend and his wife reached out to me. Mark and Patty were not my best friends then (we are now) and it surprised me that they were there for me. Their attitude was, "we're not going to choose sides", like my best friends did. Their caring support let me know I was not alone.

If you're reading my blogs, you know I got through those lonely times and went on to a happy life.

Some people feel lonely even though they have many friends. Loneliness is a form of depression. If there are times you feel lonely talk to someone. Don't let it linger because it could become a chronic problem if you procrastinate. That someone should not be your friend or family because they won't understand. They'll tell you they love you and you shouldn't feel this way. Talking to someone who has been there and recovered will help. Talking to someone who is trained to help you will also help. I prefer someone who's been there.

The worst thing you can do is try to stop yourself from feeling lonely or blue. Your body/brain is telling you something. It could be a chemical problem or a physiological problem. It could be minor or serious. Don't try to ignore it—don't try to stop it—talk to someone.

That someone might help you focus on what you have, not what you don't have. That someone would remind you to acknowledge the people who love you, the good things you have done in your life, the things and people that bring you positive energy into your life, the people who will help you define a positive future and to start doing things that are fun and make you laugh.

It could take you an hour, a week, a month or a year to get over that lonely/blue feeling. The amount of time it takes is not important. What's critical is you don't give up. What's critical is you believe this too will pass. What's critical is you trust the person you're talking to and listen to what he or she says.

Life is great. Living life is fabulous. You have a lot of living life left. During your life you'll have ups and downs. If everything was perfect in life it would be a boring life.

Going through the thrill of victory and the agony of defeat and then coming out the other side a happy person, is a fantastic life.

BLOG# 60

You Can't Always Get What You Want

Do you believe you can't always get what you want, but if you try, you might get what you need! I do! I always say: "ask for what you want, but don't demand it." I also believe you should keep asking and not give up if you don't get what you want the first time.

I also believe if you keep trying you might just get what you need. What is your definition of "need?" Do you truly know the difference between "want" and "need?" Most of the things we want are not the things we need. To have a happy life you need to focus on the things you need first. When you've gotten those need things accomplished then you can try to get the things you want.

Another way of saying the same thing is, getting what you want should be the bonus to your happiness—getting what you need is required for your happiness. The problem is most people define their needs as wants. You need a car if your job requires one. However, you don't need a fifty thousand dollar car.

You want love in your life, but you need to love yourself first. You want bling, fancy clothes and expensive food, however, all you need is, food to eat, air to breathe and shelter everything else is cosmetic. You want the outside world to say you're good enough, but you need to accept you *are* good enough no matter what the outside world thinks.

I just got back from Vegas. I didn't get what I wanted (the million dollar jackpot). However, I did get what I needed for my happiness, which was a lot of fun.

I love getting what I want. I will never stop asking for what I want because of one important thing:

I deserve it!!!!

BLOG# 61

Retirement

Is it too soon to think about retirement? Yes for some, no for others. Too many people never make a retirement plan. I'm not talking about financial planning. What I know about financial planning is save some money, don't invest in risky investments, don't buy things you can't afford and don't get divorced.

As you can see, I don't have a lot to offer you regarding your financial retirement planning. I do have knowledge in physical, emotional and happiness retirement planning. I do know when you should start planning your retirement and when you shouldn't think about it.

First let's start with the definition of retirement:

"Withdrawal from one's position or occupation or from an active working life."

Sooo, according to Webster, it's all about leaving your job and never working again. That's not my definition. My definition is:

"Stop doing the things you don't like doing and start doing the things that make you happy."

I hated getting up to an alarm clock. Now, I'm retired, I wake up when my body decides to wake up. I never liked being in meetings with too many people, none of whom could make a decision. Now that I'm retired, almost all of my meetings are one on one. I never liked the stress of having to perform or, worse yet, counting on others to perform. Now that I'm retired, I decided to never manage another living soul. I never liked having lunch or dinner with customers or management who were boring, only talked about work related things and cared only about their careers. Now that I'm retired, I only have lunch or dinner with people who are interesting and make me happy.

When I was planning my retirement, I thought about the things I wanted to do, not just the things I no longer wanted to do. I wanted to finish my second book and write my third (blogging came later). I always wanted to play the guitar. I wanted more time to mentor people. I wanted to have more time to work out. I wanted to have a dog.

I have done all the things I wanted to do and stopped doing the things I didn't want to do. As you can see, some of the things I wanted to do are work related. It takes work to write, learn the guitar, care for a dog and work-out. Therefore, Webster's definition is wrong.

In my definition, when you retire, you can take a different job if the new one is more fun than the other one. The goal is different. You do your current job for money or other reasons. The retirement job is for happiness even if you don't make a dime.

Sooo, when should you start your physical, emotional and happiness retirement planning? If you're under 40 years old, I suggest you don't even think about retirement. The reason is you're on the front side of your life's journey. You're still learning what you like and what you don't like. You're still finding new fun things to do. You might love the new experiences your current job is giving you. I was learning the computer, software and network business and that was a great deal of fun. Your social life is either blooming or going down the toilet.

At 40 you should be planning your retirement. I know it's at least twenty years away, but if you don't know where you're going, you'll never get there. Sit down and write all the things you want to change about your current life. Sit down and write down the things you never had time before to accomplish. Sit down and write all the fun things you want to do when you retire.

This list is your retirement happiness guide. Every year look at it and decide if you want to make any changes. These are going to be your golden years. The reason they're called "golden" is because these retirement years are supposed to meet the "gold" standard. My "gold" standard is to get all the happiness I can squeeze out of the years I have left.

I actually know people who are not happy after they retire. They're bored, unmotivated and no longer feel productive. They believe they're too old to get a job or do something new. They retired without a plan. One of them spent a large portion of his retirement money and opened a Taco Bell. Six months later he was miserable working too many hours and managing people who were just going through the motions.

Happiness is the forgotten ingredient of life. Your goal is happiness. Retirement can either enhance that goal or take some of the happiness out of your life. Don't wait until it's too late.

You do have control of your happiness and you do have control of what you do in your retirement.

BLOG# 62

Sweet Summertime

Remember the days in the sweet summertime, when you were a young adult, working on mysteries without a care in the world. Remember the days in the sweet summertime when you were in the back of your car using your best night moves with your girlfriend or boyfriend. Remember the days in the sweet summertime when you were humming your favorite song while being restless and board. Remember the days in the sweet summertime when you were willing to take a risk because you felt you didn't have that much to lose.

Do you remember those days or are you living those days today? I remember those days—especially the part about being in the back seat of a sixty two Chevy. The car was owned by the butcher I worked for who let me use it. At eighteen I didn't have a clue, but I was having a lot of fun trying to figure it out.

Those were the fabulous days before serious work, marriage and family had a grip on me. Two years later I was at the "End Of My Innocence." However, I'm really lucky I had those early days. I look back on them with a huge smile on my face. When I see an old Chevy, positive energy enters my brain.

If you've never experienced those days talk to people who have. Live those good times through the experiences of your friends and family. Watch movies like: "Ferris Buellers Day Off," "Breakfast Club" and "Risky Business." The goal is to focus on a happier time even if it's through others.

If you're having those days today, appreciate them. Don't take them for granted because there will be a day when you'll need to look back on them with a smile on your face.

If you lived those days, take a step back and remember them. That was a time when life was simpler, stress was a lot less, responsibilities were limited and you were humming your favorite song while being restless and board.

The most important part was when you were willing to take a risk because you felt you didn't have that much to lose. Remember when you were a risk taker (or at least less risk adverse than today). Remember when you didn't think before you acted. Remember when you did things on a dare. Remember when you fell in love (or at least in lust) every time you met someone new. Remember the summers when you were free.

The reason we don't have those days today (unless you're a teenager reading my blog) is because we believe we have too much to lose. Holding on to things is our addiction. Not willing to pay the price for taking risks is our addiction. Not willing to fall in love because we were hurt before, is our addiction. Not willing to tell people how you really feel, is our addiction. Not willing to cry is our addiction.

If you want a happier life you have to be willing to say "what the f..k" I'm going to do what I want. What's the worst that can happen? I'm willing to pay the price. "I'm mad as hell and I'm not going to take it anymore." I'm not as happy as I deserve so what do I have to lose.

The more you hold on to things the harder it is to be happy. The more things you feel you can't to lose, the harder it is to find happiness. Back in the day we didn't know any better. We were:

Working on our night moves
In the sweet summertime

BLOG# 63

It's Not The End

I was reading my Townhome newsletter today and it started with the following saying:

"Everything will be all right in the end
So if it's not all right now,
It's not the end."

I love that saying. I don't know who wrote it, but it says a lot. What it means to me is, no matter how bad things are today, it's not the end and therefore, things will get better in the future. A negative person might read that same saying and think it says, everything is shit today and because it's not the end it will only get worse. What do you think it says?

If you believe it's the former, you're reading my blogs and you get it. You're probably happy most of the time.

You probably give positive energy out to the universe. You probably are getting some mentoring or seeking it. You probably hang out with happy people. You probably make your friends happy.

You probably get what you need and try to get what you want, but don't demand it. You probably accept what's happening to you right now, but believe you can change it for the better. You probably believe life is great and want as much life as you can get. You probably believe you deserve a happy life because you've paid your dues. You probably love yourself just a little bit more than anyone and anything else in this world.

If you assume this saying means everything is shit today and because it's not the end it will only get worse, you probably are an unhappy person. You probably hang out with unhappy people. You probably don't believe life is a journey where some things that happen are good and some things that happen are bad, but either way you plan to enjoy the journey. You probably believe what comes after this life has got to be better than this one.

What if a higher being told you this is as good as it gets? What if a higher being told you after this you go to ashes or in the ground? What if a higher being told you the end is near? Would you just be miserable the remaining years of your life?

I want to believe there is something better after this. However I have set my mind to believe this is as good as it gets and if something better happens after I'm gone, that's a bonus. I want to believe my soul will still be alive after I'm dead and resurface in another life, but just in case, I believe I'm going to ashes. I want to believe I will live forever, but I know I'm going to die in the year 2038.

Wanting life after death to be special is good, but that's no way to live life today. Because I believe the end is near and there might be nothing after it ends, I focus on my happiness now. I do the things I can do today to make me happy. I attack life and try to get everything I can out of it. I'm willing to risk everything to make me happy today.

I say what I want to say and don't worry what others think. I do what I want to do knowing that the people who care for me like what I'm doing. I believe money is freedom of choice not for showing off. I buy less stuff. I eat, drink and be merry at low cost happy hour bars with my friends. I have lived in the same house for 30 years. I only hang out with the people I like. I make sure my needs are gotten. I root for happiness for the ones I care about. I do my part to make them happy and I believe I deserve all the good things that are happening to me.

The bottom line is, I just don't want to be unhappy the rest of my life while counting on life being better after I die. If today is not all right, It's OK because:

It's Not The End!!!!

BLOG# 64

Emotional Rescue

What do you do when you realize a close friend, spouse or family member is an emotional wreck? What do you want others to do if *you* are an emotional wreck? The answer to the first question is the answer to the second question.

When I completed a year and a half of therapy/mentoring I felt like I had a gift. I finally understood what was happening to me and the things I had to do and believe in to create a happier career and life for myself. I was so happy I was on the right path; I wanted to help others to get on the same path. It didn't work.

I could see the telltale signs of other people's problems with their happiness. I could see it in their words, body language and outlook on life. They were me before I saw the light. Their problems were my problems even though they acted them out differently than I. All I wanted to do was give them the light I had received. WOW was I wrong.

They didn't see me as a disinterested third party (like my mentor was to me). They saw me as their friend, family or spouse. They felt I was judging them. They believed their problems were different than my problems. They didn't believe I or anybody else could change their lives. They believed if the outside world would just stop making them unhappy their lives would be better.

Their position took me back. I had something wonderful and wanted them to have the same. Why would they feel this way? I had to realize it didn't matter what I had or believed—what mattered was what they wanted out of life. It didn't matter what I said—what mattered was what they heard. It didn't matter that I wanted to help—what mattered was did they want help.

Once I came to this realization, I stopped trying to fix everybody. Instead, I became a mentor to people who tried other solutions and still were not happy. These people were not friends, family or spouse. They saw me as a third party who only cared about their happiness. I charged them a very small amount of money for the purpose of making sure they had a stake in their transformation. The money was less than the cost of a tee shirt, but the act of writing me a check or handing me cash assured our relationship was professional.

After getting references from people I helped, the need to charge went away. I decided I would only take on people who, I believed, I could help and who truly wanted to change the path they were on. I also decided I didn't want this to become a business. All I want to do is help people. Seeing someone get it, overcome their problems and become a happier person puts a big smile on my face.

I now realize I'm doing this as much for my happiness as their happiness. Listening to what they're going through is a clear reminder of what I went through. They're actually helping me to never go back to the old Kenny.

Watching them act out is extremely interesting to me. No two clients act out their unhappiness, frustration, anger and negative energy the same way. However, what I've learned is the core of their problem is the same for all, including me. My focus is to get them to "see" the core issues that are holding them back.

If you know someone who is not happy with their life, don't talk—listen. They need a shoulder to cry on. They don't need anybody telling them what to do. They don't need someone to judge them. They don't need someone to say: "pull yourself up man and just get over it." They do need your positive energy. They do need your understanding. They do need you to tell them you love them just the way they are.

Pointing them to a disinterested third party when you believe they're ready to reach out for help is a good thing. My favorite place to go to is:

KenKenny.com

BLOG# 65

Bucket List

What the hell is a bucket list? It's a list of things you want to do before you die. That's a good thing—right? Not necessarily. It depends if it's a list of things you *want* to do or a list you *have* to do. It depends if it's a list of things that make you happy or a list that feeds your ego, gets you more money and/or enables you to control your outside world.

I don't have a bucket list. The reasons are:

- I believe I'm going to live until the year 2038, but what if I'm wrong. I could get hit by a bus right after I publish this blog. What good is a bucket list if the bucket is going to be empty by the time you read this blog?

- I like living life hour by hour, day by day, year by year, etc. My list starts when I wake up. First,

I'm thankful that I woke up and second, once I realize I'm alive, I decide what I want to do that day.

You might believe there are things you *have* to do any given day, but it's not true. You can do whatever you want to do as long as you're willing to deal with what *might* happen if you don't do what you believe you have to do.

Do you have to go to work—no? You can take the day off as long as you're willing to accept the risk (or the blessing) of getting fired. You may prefer to go to work because you like your job or because you like the money it gives you so you can enjoy your life after work.

Don't try to convince yourself there are things in life you *have* to do. When you feel you have to do something, you lose control. When you feel you have to do something, you'll eventually begin to resent the things you have to do. When you feel you have to do something, you'll get angry and frustrated.

You don't have to do anything you don't want to do. However, there might be a price to pay. If you put yourself in first position, you should only be doing the things that make you happy or lead to your happiness. You don't have to go to work, unless you like the things work gives you. You don't have to stay married as long as you're willing to deal with the emotional and financial problems that will occur. You don't have to fix the plumbing as long as you're willing to deal with the leak. You don't have to make your kids happy unless it makes you happy to see that smile on their faces

I could go on and on, but I think you get the point.

- I don't want a bucket list of wants or haves because, by definition, that list is things to do before I die. When you have a bucket list you believe you have all the time in the world to get to the list. Therefore, the list will stop you from doing those things NOW. NOW is critical. "I'm going to do" doesn't work.

Not doing NOW makes you feel you missed something. You could start feeling bad about yourself because you're procrastinating. Time is not on your side. Therefore, the best way to not feel bad is to *not* have a bucket list. Instead, have a today list.

If you're anal and have to have a bucket list, make sure it's a list of wants not haves. Make sure it's a list of preferences not demands. Make sure the items in the list are only things that will lead to your happiness.

Make sure you will love yourself even if you don't complete the list before you die.

BLOG# 66

Security and Fear

Security comes in different flavors. Some of us are addicted to financial security. Some of us are addicted to emotional security. Some of us are addicted to physical security. Some of us are addicted to all three.

Some of us would say they're not addicted to any of these, however they prefer one or more of them. Therefore, it's a matter of degree? It depends on how security affects your life and your happiness. It depends if your need for security is out of fear. It depends if your need for security is because you believe you're not capable of protecting yourself. It depends on the amount of security you feel you must have.

Needing security out of fear is the most insidious. I can't leave my husband because I fear I won't be able to have my own life without him. I can't leave my wife because she will take me for everything I've worked for. I can't leave my wife because the kids might hate me. I can't leave my husband because I'm too old to start over again.

I have to keep working because I need more money just in case I get ill. I have money, but I need more just in case a disaster occurs—I could lose it all. I'm not going to do the things I love because I must have that money for when I get old.

I'm getting a big dog and an expensive security system because someone might break into my house and rape or kill me. I'm going to spend money I could use for things that make me happy, to buy a lot of insurance just in case there is an earthquake. I'm going to spend money I could use for things that make me happy, to buy life insurance so my kids will have a lot of money when I die.

Security is practical. It's important to have financial security, but how much? I retired early to live a happier life. I have enough money for my wife and me to live comfortably, not extravagantly. I didn't need to work longer to have more money that will just be left to others (including my kids) when we die. The kids will make their own way like my wife and I have made our own way. The stress of one more day of work was not worth me having more money in my savings account so I could feel more secure.

It's important to have insurance for things like your car and your house, but do you really need to spend too much money on insurance for your jewelry? What if you lose one of your rings—will your life change? Will you be an unhappy person the rest of your life? If the answer is yes—get help now!

What are the odds that someone will break into your house and kill you? Do you really believe an expensive security system will stop someone who is on drugs and crazy or a professional house burglar? Forget the alarm system. Just get a security sign and put it out front and in the back of the house. That sign alone will get someone to look for another house. Also, forget about what the burglar might take. The goal is to protect yourself not your stuff. Therefore, get a security door in a place in your house where you can lock yourself in just in case of a fire.

What are the odds that an earthquake will destroy your house and everything in it? Not high enough to protect everything. It's practical to get enough earthquake insurance to replace your house, however all the other stuff can be replaced over time. More insurance will not protect the things that have sentimental value. In the rare case where an earthquake destroys all your stuff, life is still good and worth living. It will be hard, but you can still have a happy life if you want to.

We all want security, but it should never stand in the way of your happiness. Without it there is a risk, but you will survive. Living in a bubble of security is not a great life. Spending too much money on security instead of using that money for happiness is not going to enrich your life.

Nobody can be completely safe emotionally, financially or physically. Don't live like something bad is just around the corner.

Live life like something good will happen even if something bad is happening right now.

BLOG# 67

Teach Best What You Most Need To Learn

Last night I was watching the mind numbing, intellectually empty, stupid and totally ridiculous TV series Dallas. Believe it or not, there was a line in the show that made sense. It came from a teacher at a drug treatment center who said to another teacher *"teach best what you most need to learn."*

That's me in spades. My books, lectures, mentoring and these blogs are as much for me as they are for the people I'm sharing with. Everything I say on happiness is something I need to remember myself. Many times I write something or say something that surprises me because it's something I never thought about myself.

I watch people acting out their problems and many times I see myself, years ago, playing the same tune.

Trying to make those people better has made me better and happier over the years. Every day I think about what I'm going to blog. The answer comes when I look inside myself. Where is my happiness coming from? What could I do today to create a happier life for myself? What's missing? What's holding me back?

When I *"see"* the answers to those questions, I write a blog. My hope is those blogs will not only make me feel better and happier, but will make the people who read my work feel better and happier. When I get positive feedback, I feel great. Not because of my ego—that was lost a long time ago. It's because someone benefited from my problem resolutions.

Some of you have learned from your mistakes in life. Some of you have found a way to put some happiness in your life. Some of you need others to help you put happiness in your life. Some of you are willing to share what you've learned in life with others. Some of you are good at teaching and some of you are not.

If you're willing to share your successes with someone, remember the saying above "teach best what you most need to learn." Before you speak, look inside at the things you've overcome. Look inside at the things you're still struggling to overcome. Giving someone your insight on what problems you had in life and how you overcame them, will reinforce ***your*** accomplishments.

Letting others *"see"* the issues you're working to overcome will help you stay in tune with the work you still have to do. Keeping all this good stuff and not so good stuff to yourself will not help you become better and happier.

Take a risk for your own good. Communicate what you most need to learn. You'll be shocked at the outcome. You'll be better and happier and the person you're sharing with will be better and happier.

Never forget: Happiness Is The forgotten Ingredient In Life. That's your goal. "Teaching best what you most need to learn," is one of many ways to reach that goal.

BLOG# 68

Politics

Can politics affect your happiness? It depends on how much you give a shit. I'm a social Democrat and a fiscal Republican. I'm your typical middle of the roader. I have a big problem with the group that's strongly to the left and have the same problem with the group that's strongly to the right.

I follow politics and care about their affect and effect on the country I love. I vote my voice at the risk I will be called for jury duty. However, I don't let what's happening politically affect my mood, my behavior, my love for life, my love for country and my happiness.

I'm watching the news today and can't believe the jubilation and the deep anger over the Supreme Court Decision on health care. This ruling has brought out deep positive and negative feelings within some people. I heard people say they want conservative Chief Justice

Roberts (who placed the deciding vote) dead. I heard people say this decision is the best thing that has ever happened to them.

What if the decision went the other way? What if the Democrats win the election? What if the Republicans win the election? Do you really believe America will go under? Do you really believe your life will turn to euphoria or crap? Do you really believe these decisions will make your children's' lives a disaster?

America has been through a lot worse than the decisions stated above. We as a people always find a way to make things right over time. As bad as the system is, it's the best one available and it works—over time. No political decision will destroy you, your family, your friends, your children or your country. It's a cycle. When the country goes in the wrong direction too long, we change it.

If the Democrats win and screw things up we'll change it. If the Republicans win and screw things up we'll change it. If the health care law makes things worse, we'll change it. Everything in our country will eventually change for the good. The reason is because, in the final analysis, both parties want the best for the country and the American people. You may like or not like their politics, but that's the purpose of your vote.

Making yourself depressed, angry, frustrated and unhappy over political decisions is never going to help you find happiness (remember that's your goal). Believe in the future. Believe you and others have the power to change things for the better—over time. Accept what is happening for now and add your voice in the future.

There are so many things going on around us that affect our happiness if we let it happen. Politics is just one of them. Be involved, but not to the extent you let it shape your happiness. Feel good that you voiced your opinion, but don't demand others to feel the same as you. Feel good that you care, but take a step back if it doesn't go your way. Focus on your happiness not your politics.

I have a friend who has very different political views than I. We really go at each other when we have a political debate. However, we hug each other when it's over because we care more for each other than our political differences. No matter what political decisions politicians make we will still be friends.

Friendship is happiness. Political decisions are just political decisions that will always change over time. You have a choice.

Focusing on your happiness is always the right choice.

BLOG# 69

Electronics And Happiness

Like it or not, electronics are part of your life. Your choices are: you can decide to love electronics and all the wonderful new things they bring to your life, accept electronics into your life and use them to your advantage or hate or be afraid of electronics and do everything you can to avoid them.

I'm a lover of electronics. They have made my life better and happier. I can't wait until creative future thinking companies come out with something that will make me even happier. My wife started out being afraid of electronics. However, she's really smart and she eventually accepted them into her life. Now, she's a PC junkie. Now, she wants a car that has every electronic gadget she can afford. Now, she has a smart phone that has improved her life. She bought an iPad for Christmas.

Are you still holding on to your flip phone? Do you avoid texting? Do you still lug a camera around when you're on vacation? Does your car have a back-up camera? Do you still use a Thomas Guide when you want to go somewhere you've never been before? Do you email reluctantly? Are you aware that almost everything in your home and your car has electronics in them?

The older generation feels bad that kids today don't talk to each other, in person, face to face. However, what they don't realize is the kids today communicate more to each other than any generation has ever done before. Email and texting has enabled people to share their feelings much more than they would do so face to face. They have a nonthreatening way of saying what's really going on inside them.

The devices that let you see and talk to people over the internet have brought distant family and friends closer together. I would hardly see my son, his wife and my grandchildren if it weren't for Skype. It's not as good as being there, but it's a lot better than not seeing them at all.

Electronics enable you to stay in touch with the world instantaneously. It's not critical, but it sure makes you feel more involved. When I'm away, knowing the Dodgers' score inning by inning is not critical, but it does make me happy.

I'm reading more than I've ever read before since I bought a Kindle. I hated carrying around books. I hated folding down pages to tell me where I left off. I hated trying to find the books on the subjects I liked. The Kindle solves all those problems. If you're one of those people who say you like the feel of holding a book, get over it. Try a Kindle, it's only $79. You'll save that much in book prices in less than a year.

I have a bad back and neck. Backing out or parking my 2006 350Z was difficult and dangerous. I traded the Z for a new base model Honda CRV. One reason I chose that car was because it came with a back-up camera. Being higher in this SUV with a back-up camera makes me feel safer and that makes me happier.

There are so many new electronics coming to your TV set. Not just stuff like 3D, but electronics that will enable you to talk to people while you're watching a program, buy a product when you see a commercial, turn on or off lights, pop your popcorn, read about Paris when you're watching a movie shot in that city. I could go on and on, however the most important part is these capabilities can enrich your life if you love or embrace them into your life.

This is not me telling you to join the modern age. This is me telling you to join today's age. The modern age has yet to come. Electronics will enable us to evolve in a positive way just as the car, electric lights and your toilet have enriched your life.

Don't be afraid of electronics and what they might bring. The free market will sort out the bad stuff from the good stuff. See them for what they are—devices to make you happier. Try all of the electronics you can afford. It may take you time to make them do what you want them to do, but once you get it you'll never let them go.

Take a step back and think about how electronics have made things better for you. Appreciate them as you would appreciate anything in your life that makes you happier.

Appreciation is one of the core elements of happiness. Electronics is just one of many things you should be appreciating about your life.

The more things you appreciate the happier you become. The happier you become the more you appreciate the things in your life. The happiness circle goes round and round.

BLOG# 70

Always Make Something Good Out Of Something Bad

My wife's uncle Charles would say: *"always make something good out of something bad."* I knew he was right, but it's really hard to accomplish. We look at things as good or bad. Many times we don't appreciate the goods things and many times we focus too much on the bad things.

Not taking a step back and appreciating the good things will retard your happiness. Focusing on the bad things will destroy your happiness. The answer is obvious for what to do with the good things, however not as obvious as to what to do with the bad things.

For example, how do you make something good out of a broken leg? The answer is to first stop being upset that you broke your leg. You need to stop being angry because you feel you could have avoided breaking your leg in the first place. No shouldas or couldas. Stop being frustrated with the limitations a broken leg will mean to your everyday life. The leg is broken—deal with it.

After you've accepted your beautiful broken leg, make a list of what good could happen because your leg is broken. Now, you can get on an airplane before everybody else. Now, you can have your friends and family take care of you instead of you always taking care of them. Now, you can get everybody together to sign your wonderful cast. Now, you can get out of work or school early (or not go at all). Now, you can do the quiet things (like reading or watching TV shows) that you seem to never have the time to do. Now, you can build up your arm muscles getting around on those fantastic crutches.

If you focus on making something good out of a broken leg, your frustration and anger will lessen. Less frustration and anger—more happiness. More happiness will make it seem like your leg is healing faster. The faster you feel your leg is healing, the more positive outlook you'll have. The more positive outlook—the more happiness.

Let's take on a more difficult bad thing. Your spouse leaves you or your boyfriend/girlfriend leaves you or your best friend no longer has your back or your family starts treating you like crap. Making something good out of those bad things is difficult, but not impossible. I know because I lived it.

As I stated before, you have to first start accepting this has happened to you. No more blaming them or most importantly blaming you. That's very hard and probably will take time, but it's a must if you're going to recover. Thinking about what good you can make out of this bad will help you get over it faster.

Sooo, what good can come from this disaster? Maybe for the first time in a long time you're free to do the things you like to do without getting approval from another person. Maybe for the first time in a long time you're free to meet new friends who are not part of your old clan. You'll eventually meet someone else who will be more interesting, more fun, accepts you just the way you are and gives you more freedom than you had before. Maybe for the first time in a long time you'll be alone with yourself and find out you want someone in your life, but don't ***need*** someone to make you happy.

Maybe you'll find out the person who left you weren't the right person in the first place. Maybe you'll find out the friend who didn't have your back was not the friend you thought he or she was in the first place. Maybe you'll realize you never did need those family members who don't love you.

Bad things are always going to happen in your life. Making something good out of something bad will build your self-confidence. Making something good out of something bad will help you like yourself more. Making something good out of something bad will be positive energy. Making something good out of something bad will tell your friends and family you have your act together. Making something good out of something bad will get your friends and family to consider how they should act when they have something bad happen to them.

When your friends and family make something good out of something bad, they bestow positive energy on you. Positive energy will encourage you to make something good out of your something bad.

Positive energy begets positive energy. Positive energy begets happiness. Happiness is the forgotten ingredient of life.

Be the source of positive energy by making something good out of something bad.

BLOG# 71

Is There Life On Mars?

Is there life on Mars? Was there ever bacteria life on Mars? Why do I give a shit? How will my life change for the better if we find bacteria on Mars? Is there life on other planets in the universe? With trillions of planets going around a crap load of suns, the very strong odds say yes. Therefore, why do we have to search for them? ***Let them find us***.

As you know from my blog on "Electronics and Happiness", I'm all in favor of using space or physics to discover new things that will improve our lives here on earth. There are very critical minerals on our Moon. These minerals can be used to enhance or create capabilities, here on Earth, which will make life better for all of us. Spending money to go to the Moon and bring them back could be a good value to mankind.

Spending billions maybe trillions of dollars on trying to find life on a distant planet makes no sense to me. There are very rich people, organizations and companies that want the answer. Therefore, I say, ***let them pay for the answer***.

What does my government have to do with it? What's it their business? The government's role is to spend my money on things that will enrich our lives. Finding bacteria on Mars will do no such thing. Finding a cure for cancer is a much better investment by the government than spending billions to see if, on a galaxy far, far away, someone is watching TV.

It amazes me that we're not standing outside Washington with signs saying:

"Star Trek Has Already Given Us The Answer."

"New Roads and Bridges Yes—New Frontiers No."

"Cure Alzheimer, Not Mysteries Of The Universe."

"Feed The Poor, Not NASA."

"Make A Movie, Not A Spacecraft."

"I've Already Seen Them—Just Take My Word For It."

We have grown up in a world where books and movies have tantalized our imagination about life on other planets. I grew up with "ET", "Close Encounters Of The Third Kind", "The Day The Earth Stood Still," etc. I always wanted to be an Astronaut. I would be the first in line to take a trip to another planet and I probably would still be first today.

However, now I'm retired and the government is considering reducing my Medicare. I've lost dear friends to Cancer and AIDS. I'm watching the infrastructure in LA deteriorate. I'm talking to people I care about, struggling to find a job. I'm watching my taxes being spent on a few Mars rovers digging up dirt.

Why is this happening? The answer is the usual—follow the money. Government is not always practical or logical, however they are always political. Someone a lot richer than us wants this to happen. Scientists always want to explore, but I don't see them putting their money where their mouths are.

I do want to know the answer to life. I do want to know if we are alone. However, I want safety, health and happiness more. I know our government's money could be spent to make me healthier and happier. If they just took half the many trillions of dollars being spent on space exploration five things would happen:

1. Yes, it would take longer to find the mysteries of the universe. Why do I care if it takes a hundred years or two hundred years to find these answers—I'm not going to be around and neither are you!

2. I might not die of Cancer, Alzheimer, heart disease, diabetes, etc. if the government would stop mapping Saturn.

3. I would not be afraid to travel over the Brooklyn Bridge if the government used my money to fix infrastructure and create more jobs.

4. My Grandchildren would go to better schools if our government cared as much about education as they care about whether there ever was water on Mars.

5. I would be safer and happier because the government would spend my money on safety and other programs that would enrich our lives.

Number five is what I want my government to do for me. I realize I can't count on the outside world (in this case the government) to make me happy, but as my father would say:

"It wouldn't hurt."

BLOG# 72

Madoff

What a sad time in our history. What Madoff did went beyond any robbery in our history. Previous robberies and scams affected relatively few people. Some could actually afford the loss. This disaster ruined thousands of people's lives.

Yes, there were some greedy people who knew it was too good to be true. I don't feel so bad for them. However, most of the people were naive to what was going on, trusted Madoff like they trusted their favorite family member, were part of an investment group, like a stock fund, and had no idea where the fund was investing their money or they were part of a retirement fund that had control of their retirement money.

These people, through no fault of their own, lost almost everything. Some of these people are so old they have to count on family and friends to get them through the day. Some, who were planning their retirement, now have to work beyond their golden years.

Is Madoff paying for his sins? Many would say no. Yes he's lost his freedom, but the same people he screwed are paying for his prison room and board with their tax dollars. Is he an unhappy person—I sure hope so. He has the burden of not only screwing other people, he has taken everything from his wife and children and their children. His son committed suicide because he couldn't face prison or the wrath of the thousands he hurt. If Madoff is not unhappy then he truly is a monster.

Well, so far this blog is a major downer. However, you know me: "Always Make Something Good Out Of Something Bad." The great majority of these victims are still alive. If they are, they have food to eat, air to breath and shelter. They may have found out who their real friends and family are. They may have found a job they like. They may have found peace within themselves.

This was a great loss, but an earthquake, fire or tornado could have done the same. It's just easier to hate an individual than hate Mother Nature. We know we don't have control of Mother Nature. We assume the earth and the weather have a mind of their own. However, we feel we should have been able to control our investments. Yes, Madoff was a dog, but why didn't I see it? How could I have been so stupid? Why would he do this to me?

You see, what's worse than losing everything is focusing on your mistakes in life. What's worse than losing all your money, is being angry with yourself afterward. What's worse than losing all your money, is getting so depressed you stop loving life. What's worse than losing all your money, is letting Madoff take away your happiness.

I lost almost all my money twice through divorce. I survived. I found friends and family who stood up for me. I stopped being angry with my ex-wives. I accepted what happened and started my new journey. I didn't see the situation as someone taking everything away from me. I saw the situation as shit happens and I'm not going to let life pass me by.

I'm heartfelt at the loss these people have endured. I know it was not their fault. I know they were taken by a greedy, uncaring piece of crap. However, I also know life is great. There are so many good things that can still happen to these people if they want it bad enough. I know anger is not the answer to their happiness.

I can only hope these victims don't hate themselves. I can only hope they find a way to continue to reach for all the happiness that's still available to them. They deserve it!!

BLOG# 73

Sue Baby Sue

If you watch TV you most likely have seen the ads for a number of law firms. They boast a super high success rate and have gotten their clients millions of dollars. Isn't that great! Well, NO! Who do you think is paying for those hundreds of millions of dollars—YOU!

Let's take a look at their success rate. I would guess ninety percent are settled before it goes to court. I would guess they convince their clients to accept a deal that's much less than their client would get if it went to trial. I would guess they prey on poor people who are really damaged, but need money now. I would guess they accept frivolous lawsuits they believe they can settle in a very short time.

To keep me from being sued, these are my opinions and have zero facts behind them. You should make up your own mind.

We are a litigious country. Many of the lawsuits are necessary and protect us from harm or pay us for the damage done. However, there are too many (in my opinion) lawsuits that are done out of anger, greed and revenge.

How many divorces could be settled by two adults who respect each other enough to sit down and work out a fair deal for both—A LOT. The stress of fighting to make sure you get more than he or she is just not worth it. The anger to get back at someone because they hurt you is just not worth it. What about the other people who suffer (like the kids)? Do either of you care enough about them to settle without a prolonged legal fight? Do you really feel better and happier because you took him or her for everything they had? If you do, you're not reading my blogs.

I left my first wife with three thousand dollars and a beat-up old car. I wanted my freedom more than I wanted a fight. I cared more for the kids then I cared for the money. I believed I would recover and make the money back. I left my second wife because of emotional stress. She sued me for everything and I gave it to her. My choice was to spend all my money having lawyers fight the divorce to the death (as she was willing to do) or give her the house, cars and money so I could go on with my life. Just the stress relief was worth the price. Again, I recovered.

I know people who will give lawyers thousands of dollars to fight over six inches of property. Slip and fall is one of the most common lawsuits. You go into a 7-Eleven, don't notice (or do notice if you're a crook) a wet spot and slip. You sue for doctor bills plus pain and suffering. I get the doctor bills. I don't get the pain and suffering. You're not going to be handicapped the rest of your life. You're not going to be mentally ill the rest of your life. It hurt—so what? You'll get over it and life will go on.

What if you fell in your kitchen? Would you sue the linoleum for pain and suffering? No, you would accept the pain for now knowing it will be gone soon. But, why not sue 7-Eleven—they're rich. The reason is because these kinds of lawsuits force them to pay a lot for insurance and hire a legal staff. Nothing is for free—their product prices will go up because someone other than you fell on their floor.

I'm not down on lawyers (my son is a lawyer—contract law) or the people who deserve to sue. I am down on people using the legal system to make money, get revenge, make a point or, believe it or not, because they can.

We have the highest insurance rates of any country. We have the highest health costs of any country and our health care is not the best in the world. We have a stressful society because we sue too much. We take more drugs for stress than any other country.

I, for one, believe we're all in this together. Suing a company, a doctor, a candlestick maker, etc. has a negative effect on their workers, all the people who need their products and services and you.

People are suffering because of high prices. People are suffering because the cost of insurance is ridiculously high. People are suffering because they know it's so easy to get sued. We, as a community, can stop this from happening. New laws won't work because they'll hurt people who truly need the law to protect or reimburse them. New laws won't work because politics are involved. New laws won't work because too many people are getting rich with the laws just the way they are.

Therefore, it's up to us. We could go back to the way it was in this country when I was a boy. Back then, a car hits another car. The two drivers get out and scream at each other. After the screaming, they look at the damage and one pays the other. No lawsuit, no pain and suffering. They just go off and fix their bumpers.

Neighbors were neighborly back then. If they had a difference they settled it by talking to each other. No lawyers—no lawsuits—no being mad at each other—no stress. Back then, if your doctor did something wrong you stopped seeing him and told all your friends to stop seeing him. In my neighborhood we actually made a lousy dentist leave the neighborhood because nobody would go to him.

I appreciate my life today more than I did back then except for the negative energy affect today's lawsuits have on all of us.

BLOG# 74

68 And Loving It

Yesterday was my birthday. I'm 68 and loving it. When I was a kid, I believed when I got to be 68 I thought my life would be over. The family and friends I grew up with seemed old, tired, in poor health and just not loving life.

Being poor required 68 year olds to keep working in jobs their bodies were not designed to do. My grandparents didn't have pensions or Social Security. They didn't have the medicines or the cures they have today. Even if they did, they couldn't afford it. Their friends were in the same boat, so *they* didn't love life either.

Basically their life consisted of work, eat, sleep and taking a shit (which sometimes was the highlight of their day). They did enjoy their grandkids who were able to put a smile on their faces when they visited.

For some seniors today, nothing has changed. However, for many, like me, life at 68 is great and appreciated. These are my reasons for loving life in my senior years.

- My stress level is ninety percent less since I retired. I have much more control of my life. I can wake up when I want, sleep when I want, work at the things I love doing when I want, say things I truly mean, see the friends and family I want to see, go to Vegas and not be concerned bad things might be happening at work, get drunk when I want, call bullshit on people who make shit up, never have to do things or buy things just to look good to others, not get angry, frustrated or start a fight when things don't go my way or when someone intimates I'm not good enough and, best of all, have all morning to take a good crap when the urge calls for it.

- I feel safe. Medicare and my supplemental pays for all my doctor and hospital bills. I get great care and don't have to worry I could lose everything due to an illness or injury. I have a pension, Social Security and some savings. I will always have food to eat, air to breath and shelter. I don't have to worry about making ends meet. I drive a car that's safe, not flashy. I have the time to eat right, work out and generally take care of my health.

- I have great friends and family. Getting older gets you to appreciate everything more. That's especially true of friends and family. My son calls me all the time to check in. I received Happy Birthday greetings from all my friends and many other people I haven't seen in many years (Facebook rocks). I'm going to a bar tonight because friends and even the bartenders want to wish me Happy Birthday. My wife loves me and I feel her warmth deep into my heart.

- I feel great. Not so much physically, but mentally. I not only enjoy every day I wake up, I also have a positive outlook toward the future. My CEO once said to me that life is a journey not a destination. I didn't really understand him at that time, but I sure do now. I just love the journey.

I hope, when you get to 68 you'll appreciate all the things I stated above. Now that I think about it, why wait?

Why not start today appreciating everything that 68 will feel like when you get there.

BLOG# 75

Life Is Just A Bunch Of Moments

"Life is just a bunch of moments" Mel Brooks in the movie "Life Stinks"

Isn't that a great line? What a great way to view your life. Some moments are great and some moments stink. However, either way, they're just moments. Having a child is just a moment. Getting married is just a moment. Getting a divorce is just a moment. Having a fight with your friend is just a moment. Having make-up sex is just a moment.

Your life is a culmination of moments. We tend to spend more time remembering the bad moments. We too often take for granted the good moments. If you look at your life in the aggregate, I would bet that most of the people who read my blogs have had more good moments than bad moments. Therefore, most of you have had and are having a good life.

Why is it that too many of us don't look at their lives that way? Mostly because, the bad moments hurt more than the good moments feel great. Mostly, because too many of us focus on the bad moments. It's usually because we have too many friends and family who talk too much about their bad moments. It's usually because, we listen to them.

What if every time you think of a bad moment, you force yourself to think about a good moment? What if you decide to at least consider your life a push with equal good and bad moments? What if you stop describing your life as good or bad? What if you wipe away your memory and only look at your life as it is today.

If you've been reading my blogs you should know by now you have control of what you do today. Are you going to make it a good moment or are you going to make it a bad moment? Are you going to let the outside world make today a bad moment or are you waiting for *them* to make it a good moment.

What if today turns out to be a bad moment in your life? Do you believe that tomorrow will balance it out with a good moment? It's a lot easier to accept a bad day when you believe tomorrow will be better.

I think it's time you write down the culmination of your life. That's right; you need to write it down. On one side write the good moments and on the other side write the bad moments. I'm sure you'll have no problem writing down the bad moments so push yourself to remember all the good moments. Start with the big ones (like marriage, broken leg, etc.) then write down all the small ones.

What you'll find out is most of the bad moments are the big ones and most of good moments are the small ones. However, the sum of the small good moments will either balance out or overcome the bad moments.

It's critical for your happiness to view your life in the aggregate. If you do, you'll be surprised it isn't as bad as you probably think it was or is today. At worst, it will be even.

Even is great because today and tomorrow will be good moments if you want them to be.

BLOG# 76

Big Government—Small Government

Being a fiscal conservative and a social democrat puts me in a quandary as to whether I like big government or small government. I do believe our government should have a role in helping people. However, I also believe our government squanders money on things it has no business spending money on.

If we could figure out a way to balance both, we could reduce the deficit without new taxes. However, what do I want to sacrifice? More importantly, are YOU willing to sacrifice?

As you know, I'm not big on spending billions and trillions on finding life outside this earth. That wouldn't make a *huge* dent, but it's a good start. I do have a problem with the current welfare system. It encourages the wrong things. People really do have more children to get more welfare. People don't try has hard to get a job because they get welfare. People won't accept a menial job because they get welfare. People fake physical and emotional problems to get welfare. I don't have a solution on how to fix it, but somebody in government should.

We need a strong military, but how strong? Why do we spend billions on military equipment that hasn't proven itself? Like any business, the corporations should spend their money building things the government would buy. If they come up with something, they get a huge government contract and make a lot of money. Instead, the government gives these contractors billions before they even see a working model. Steve Jobs didn't expect us to pay for an iPhone before he had a finished product.

The people in Congress who make these decisions are the same people who are staunch believers in capitalism. The way the government gives money to these military contractors is not capitalism.

We give billions around the globe to people who don't even like us. I guess it's because we fear that if we don't, they'll do harm to us. Trust me; it's not working for us or for them. If we decided to give them a little less each year, they might decide to try capitalism to make their economy better. They would eventually be required to build a more democratic system where invention and innovation would be encouraged. It would lead to bright people creating products and services that their own people want. Being the welfare giver to these countries is not helping them and it sure as hell is not helping us.

Why are we the savior of the people around the world? I would love to have the money to help everyone on earth, but we don't. We have a huge deficit. Our cost of living is skyrocketing. We're talking about raising taxes. We're talking about cutting social programs, education, road and bridge construction, etc. I feel really bad for those people around the globe, but it's not our problem. Someone else has to step up for them because we have our own problems.

What the hell does this have to do with happiness—a lot! Taking away our Medicare would greatly affect millions of people. Even if the government just reduces Medicare's benefits it would be a big blow. Is anybody even thinking about not giving Medicare or Social Security to people who have adjusted gross income of over 10 million dollars?

Not funding education is a guarantee our children and their children will grow up in a have and have not society. Not funding the repair of roads and bridges guarantees our interstate commerce will greatly suffer. That would affect the Gross National Product (GNP) we produce. A lower GNP would make us a second class society.

For all of our happiness, we need to get involved. The most critical thing we have is the right to vote. Don't give up that most precious right. Don't just vote for President, vote for every office and every ballot issue. The worst that can happen is you might be called for jury duty (which is also the right thing to do and is one of the things that makes America special).

The next thing you can do is speak up.
Reach as many people as you can.
Promote your candidate.
Write A Blog!

BLOG# 77

Money Love

When it comes to money, there are things you need to consider.

You want to do good things with it.
People will lie and cheat—for the love of money.
Money can be the root of all evil if you allow it.
Money can do funny things to some people.
Some people feel they got to have it.
Some people feel they really need it.
I say, don't let money rule you.
I say, don't let money fool you.
I say, don't let money change you.

Most people don't want to do bad things to get money. Most people don't want to do bad things with the way they use money. However, how many of you want to do good things with it? Giving money to get a tax deduction or giving money because you were invited to a charitable event is not really doing good things if you don't care about the cause.

Thinking about how you plan to use your money to do good things and then executing the plan is right. Knowing who you're giving the money to and how it will be used for the good of people or animals is right. Thinking about how you'll *benefit* from giving money for good things is wrong.

Little cheating is cheating. Stealing a little money from the government on your taxes is stealing money from most of us. Do you love that money so much you'll feel good about stealing a few hundred from the government? Do you love money so much you'll even consider not paying back a loan from a friend or a family member? Do you love money so much you would lie to a friend to get what he or she worked so hard to get.

Money is only the root of all evil if it makes you evil. Everybody should prefer to have money. In a capitalistic system money is freedom of choice. Being addicted to money will get you to do things that will affect your moral compass. You'll become the kind of person you used to hate.

I hate when people say "got to have it—really need it." If you're reading this blog you're at least middle class financially. You don't "*got to have it.*" You can build a happy and rewarding life without more than you currently have. Feeling you "got to have more" will never lead to more happiness. An addiction is something you'll never have enough of. Once you get more money you'll want even more if you're addicted to it.

Don't let money rule you, fool you or especially change you. I know it's not always fair that some people who don't deserve to have more money, have more. You're smarter, work harder and deserve more than "them." However, if you live your life happy while giving positive energy out to the universe, you don't have to have as much as them. Being jealous, angry, frustrated because they have more will mean that happiness is the forgotten ingredient in your life.

You're great just the way you are. More money will not make you greater. If the money shows up because you earned it or is given to you, you'll only be happy with the extra money if you appreciate it. You'll only be happy with the extra money if you use it for good. You'll only be happy with the extra money if you don't become addicted to it. You'll only be happy with the extra money if you don't let money change you.

Burn the following statement into your brain:

You Will Always Have Enough Money If You're Happy.
You Will Never Have Enough Money If You're Not Happy.

BLOG# 78

Physical Work Vs. Mental Work

Are you exhausted after work? Most people are. What I learned from having both physical and mental jobs is that both are demanding. However, there is one difference between the two kinds of jobs. Unless you're a manager or an owner, your physical job ends when the day is over. A mental job can stay with you after the work day ends.

When I worked in my father's small sandwich shop my chores were making sandwiches, scooping ice cream, washing dishes, taking out trash and cleaning up—a lot of cleaning up. At the end of the day, I was tired, but I felt good about the work I had done and the fact it was over. I could now play with my friends and do some homework (not a lot of homework—I hated school).

My father on the other hand, left work at the end of the day, but never felt good because he worried about: will his meats come in on time the next day, will we be busy enough to pay the bills, will the landlord raise our rent, etc. etc. etc. Yes, we both did physical work, but I was happy when the day ended my father was not.

My career led me to all mental work. I was mentally drained when my work day was over, but I loved my jobs and that made me happy. As I moved up the corporate ladder, my new mental jobs came with a lot more responsibility. Even though I loved those jobs also, I was not only spent when I got home, I worried about the things left undone. That worry took a lot of the fun out of my jobs and left me mentally exhausted.

If a plumber completes three jobs that day, he's tired, but goes home happy. The boss will tell him what jobs to go to the next day. He doesn't have to think about it until he arrives at work the next day. If the plumber owns the plumbing business, he goes home thinking about the next day, week's, etc. His day never ends.

If an accountant ends the day, he goes home thinking about all the work he has on his plate that has to be done by noon the next day. Even though he works for someone else, his day doesn't end when he gets home.

It's just my opinion (because I don't know shit) that physical workers have better family lives, divorce less and are happier overall. They may not make as much money as mental workers, but after a great hot shower, they can't wait to hug the kids.

Again, my opinion, mental workers have less happy family lives, divorce more and worry too much. After their day, they don't take a hot shower (because they showered before they went to work), they go to the bathroom with the daily paper, shut the door and unwind for at least twenty minutes. When they come out, their mind is on the work left undone which leaves little emotional time with spouse and kids.

Sooo, is the answer to quit your mental job and take a physical job? For some, that's the right answer. However, for most of us it's not an option. Therefore, what is the answer?

It all goes back to the things you've been reading about in my blogs. You're in control of your happiness. You don't have to worry about the work not finished. That's right—stop worrying. The work will be there when you show up the next day. You'll get it done on time because you're good enough.

You can take a hot shower or a fantastic dump. You can leave the bathroom and tell your spouse, kids, friends or family what a great lunch you had that day. Your job is your job. If you decide to hate it or feel exhausted by it, you won't have the emotional energy to enjoy your life. If you accept your job for what it gives you, then go home thinking about anything or everything other than your job.

Now That's The Way to Happiness.

BLOG# 79

Calling Doctor Feel Good

Unless you've had an accident, serious disease or you're the luckiest person in the world, the following rules apply:

- If you're in your mid-twenties, you've never seen a doctor and take no medications.

- If you're in your mid-thirties, you go to the doctor rarely and still don't take any medications.

- If you're in your mid-forties, you go to the doctor at least once every six months and take one or two medications.

- If you're in your mid-fifties, you go to the doctor at least every three months (including check-ups and scheduled events like a colonoscopy—UGH). You now are taking around three to five medications and vitamins.

- If you're in your mid-sixties, you're now going to multiple doctors for all kinds of stuff and you're taking at least five medications and a shit load of vitamins.

- If you're in your mid-seventies, you know the first name of all your doctors, their wife's names and the names of some of their children. You're also not sure what medications you're taking or when you're supposed to take them because you have CRS ("Can't Remember Shit").

- If you're in your mid-eighties, you're just happy to get out of bed in the morning to call doctor feel good.

The drug companies don't want us to die because they make the most money on old people. The drug companies don't want to cure anything because they won't be able to sell all the drugs that allow us to live with our problems. There isn't any money in a cure for cancer, AIDS or any other major disease.

Therefore, we are going to live longer. Get that in your head. If you're unhappy now, think about the many, many years ahead of you to still be unhappy. If you're happy now, look at all the years you still have to be happy and give happiness to others.

I take the drugs and the vitamins because I want to live as long as I can. My biggest problem with dying is I won't get to see it all. I love my cell phone and want to see what it will be like to use a phone in the distant future. I love my car and wonder if that's the way we'll get from place to place hundreds of years from now.

I love my friends and wonder if in the future, face to face conversation, hugging, kissing, intercourse, etc. will happen the way it happens today. In the Woody Allen movie "Sleeper" people used an Orgasmatron to have great sex. The individual person stepped into the device, set the strength of the orgasm and pressed go. Two minutes later they came out of the device spent.

I believe whatever the world will look like hundreds and thousands of years from now, it will be great and I want to see it. However, the drug companies are probably not going to find a way to keep me alive that long.

Sooo, since I love my life now, I'm going to do all I can to hang around as long as I can.

Calling Doctor Feel Good—Calling Doctor Feel Good—Calling Doctor Feel Good.

BLOG# 80

FYI—Smile

In my blog "Have You Laughed Today," I gave you my thoughts on why it's important to laugh. Today, I not only got confirmation that laughing is important to having a happy life, but even just a smile will reduce your stress. Less stress—more happiness.

Please read the following:

TUESDAY, July 31 (HealthDay News)—Stressed out? Turn that frown upside down and you might just feel better, new research contends.

Researchers at the University of Kansas subjected college students to anxiety-inducing tasks and found that those who smiled through them appeared to have less stress.

The study, led by research psychologists Tara Kraft and Sarah Pressman, is scheduled for publication in an upcoming issue of *Psychological Science*.

"Age-old adages, such as 'grin and bear it,' have suggested smiling to be not only an important nonverbal indicator of happiness but also wishfully promotes smiling as a panacea for life's stressful events," Kraft said in a journal news release. "We wanted to examine whether these adages had scientific merit; whether smiling could have real health-relevant benefits."

To do so, they had 169 university students engage in tasks known to induce stress, such as tracing a star using their non-dominant hand while looking at a reflection of the star in a mirror. Another task had the participants plunge their hand into icy water.

The students performed these tasks under three conditions: not smiling; being explicitly instructed to smile; and while holding chopsticks in their mouth in a way that forced the face to smile.

The researchers included the chopsticks condition because they wanted to gauge the effect of "genuine" smiling (which involves the muscles around the mouth and eyes), and so-called "standard"

smiles, which involve only the muscles around the mouth—the kind of smile induced by the chopsticks.

Kraft and Pressman used heart rate measurements and self-reported stress levels to assess how perturbed the participants were during the tasks.

The study found that participants who wore any kind of smile were less stressed during the tasks than those with neutral facial expressions, and stress levels dipped especially low for folks with "genuine" smiles.

According to the authors, this means that even forcing a smile during an unpleasant task or experience might actually lower your stress level, even if you're not feeling happy.

I know it's hard to believe you're in control of your happiness, but even the doubters can force a smile. Try it TODAY! When you get good at it you might even be able to have a genuine smile in the face of adversity.

I always said "I judge my life by the number of times I laugh." Now I can add smile to that statement. Sooo,

Smile—What's Stopping You—
Absolutely Nothing!

BLOG# 81

Lean On Me

If you don't know the song "Lean On Me" by the great writer and singer, Bill Withers, go out immediately and buy it or download it. It tells us we all have pain and sorrow, but if we're wise we'll believe there is always tomorrow.

I didn't used to believe that was true. I wasn't thinking there would always be a better tomorrow. I was just focusing on the pain and the sorrow of today. I was in a deep "why me God" frame of mind. How about you? When you have pain (physical and/or mental) or sorrow do you trust that you'll eventually get out of the funk and create a better tomorrow? I do now, but it's really tough.

The song also tells us that if you're not strong you can always lean on me. Besides me doing a "woe is me," I wasn't willing to lean on my friends. I thought that because I was sad I shouldn't make them sad. Truth be told, I used that bullshit excuse to mask my fear that they wouldn't be there for me. Not only was I in pain and sorrow, I was also very insecure about my relationships because I didn't love myself.

If I had only realized my friends wanted to be there for me, I would have gotten over those days sooner. Now that I've seen the light, I want to be there for my love ones not just because it makes me happy (which is my life goal), but because someday I might have to lean on them.

The song goes on to say that when you're going through a bad time you should swallow your pride and ask for what you need from your friends and family. If they can give you what you need, they will. If you get it from them, your problem will lessen and you'll feel loved.

However, the hardest step is being willing to "swallow your pride" and let people know what *exactly* you're going through. You won't look weak to them. You won't look insecure to them. You won't look out of control to them. If they feel any of those things, they're not a good friend in the first place. A good friend will say to you, just call on me when you need a hand because we all need someone to lean on.

I tell the people I mentor to call me anytime. I don't want them to wait for our scheduled appointment. I want them to know:

If there is problem you can't carry

I'll share your problem if you just call me

BLOG# 82

Sports

It's NFL Sunday. I'm sitting on the sofa, in my Man Cave, while my friend Hank is sitting on the chair next to me. We're both watching football on my fifty inch TV. I have the Direct TV NFL Football Package that enables me to watch all sixteen games being played that day.

Hank is a staunch New England Patriots fan and I'm a long suffering Rams fan. Hank is in a betting pool where he and his partner pick winners of each game. If he wins the pool, he and his partner get to split hundreds of dollars each week. They can win thousands if they win the whole year.

I took a different approach. I love football and I wanted to get my wife involved. She could care less about football until I suggested we bet on six games a week. Now, she has become a rabid football fan. To win thirty dollars a week (6 x $5) she has learned the game, learned the teams and screams holy hell if her team screws up.

As of this writing she's up on me by twenty dollars. Two years ago I got her for twenty dollars for the whole year. However, last year she got me for a hundred (she's really good at this).

The important thing here is now football is fun for the both of us. Football Sunday has become a special day because we both hate to lose. She doesn't have a favorite team, but she does have a few teams she hates. The only reason I can assume she hates those teams is because she loses when she bets on them.

I'm always very competitive. My wife is not because she hates to lose. However, she becomes very competitive on Football Sunday. Even though I also hate to lose, I love seeing her smile when she wins. She doesn't rub it in when I lose, but I can see how proud she is when she beats me.

I love football, but it doesn't define me. Hank loves football and buys hats, helmets, shirts and jackets that have a Patriot's logo on them. Even though he gets upset when the Patriots lose, they don't define him. My friend Kenny is a major Yankees baseball fan, but they don't define him.

I mention this because there are people who are defined by their sports team. In many countries outside the United States, football (Americans call it soccer) is a major pastime. Fans around the globe have died fighting because the home team loses to the visiting team. To those fans, football is almost a religious experience. They *are* defined by their team.

We're seeing more of this problem in America. Some people are so defined by their team they will fight someone wearing a jersey with another team's logo on it. This happens more when their favorite team loses.

Sports should be fun. Win or lose it should be entertainment. Feeling depressed, angry or frustrated, for more than a few minutes after a game, is not normal. There is something else going on inside these people than just the sport. Their team losing is just bringing out the bad stuff inside them.

Happy people don't fight, get depressed or get angry when their team loses. People who give positive energy out to the universe love the entertainment of the sport and the team they love. People who love life see sports as another positive element in their life.

Unhappy people get their negative energy button pressed when their team sucks. These are the people who need the outside world to be good to them. These are the people who don't love themselves. These are the people who blame everyone and everything for their unhappiness. These are the people who are defined not only by their sports, but by their politics, religion, etc.

Sports are important in my life. I enjoy watching my favorite football team, basketball team and sometimes baseball team. Sports make me happy. However, I'm defined by the number of times I laugh. I'm defined by the life I love. I'm defined by the positive energy I get from the universe.

I'm Defined By The Good I see In Myself And Other People.

BLOG# 83

I'm Calling Bullshit

Yesterday friends of mine invited another friend to meet at a bar. The friend sent a txt back saying: "I can't make it because I was at that bar earlier in the week and today it's too hot outside." *I'm calling bullshit!* First, I know he was at the bar earlier in the week, but he didn't drive the thirty minutes, someone else drove. Second, it's hot all over Southern California. It's hot no matter what bar he goes to. Lastly, what does hot have to do with it? He gets into an air-conditioned car, drives to the bar, valet's the car and walks eight steps into the air-conditioned bar.

Why not just say: "I love you guys, but I don't feel like going tonight. I'll see you soon." It's a simple response, easy to understand and not bullshit.

A friend buys a fairly expensive dress, puts it on and asks you how she looks. You say: "it's nice." Or you say: "I'm really not the right person to ask." Or you say: "what do

I know about expensive dresses." *I'm calling bullshit!* She looks horrible in that dress. Why not say: "Hey girl that dress makes your butt look like you stuffed a sandbag down your panties." Or you could be nicer and say: "you really don't look very good in that dress. I'd take it back and get something better for less money."

It's a simple response, easy to understand and not bullshit.

You go to an expensive restaurant and order the Chef Special. It tastes like unseasoned mush. It looks good, but it's tasteless. The Chef comes over and asks: "how is your meal." With a blank face you say: "it's nice." *I'm calling bullshit!* It's not nice. It's not even good. It's costing you a lot of money. You're the customer.

Why not say: "Chef, thanks for stopping over. Your food presentation is great, but my meal is bland and really not worthy of this great restaurant. I'm sure the other menu items are fantastic, but tonight's Chef Special is not very good."

Now, you could have said: "Chef this meal sucks and I want my money back." That's very direct, but the Chef is not your friend and it's not necessary to be so blunt to get your message across. However, it is important to tell the Chef the truth—not bullshit.

Why do we play nice and not say what we really feel? Why doesn't the person who you're giving your bullshit response, just say: "*I'm calling bullshit!*" "I know you don't want to drive to the bar. It's OK, another time." "I'm calling bullshit!" "I can see in your face you don't like my new dress. Why not just say so—I'll still love you." "I'm calling bullshit!" "The fact you have hardly eaten your meal tells me you don't like it. Why not just tell me what you think it's missing. That way I can choose if I want to fix it so other customers don't get a bad meal. Also, if you just said so, I would get you something else to eat."

Our answer is: "I don't want to hurt the person's feeling." Again, I'm calling bullshit! Giving a person honest feedback is the right thing to do. It is information they need. You have the power to say it in a way that won't get them to be defensive. If they're a close friend, just tell them like it is—they'll still be your friend.

Saying you didn't want to hurt their feelings, is really about you being concerned they won't like you anymore. Not wanting to create conflict is you not being secure enough to share your true feelings. You know your friend will not leave you. Even if they get pissed off because you said something they didn't want to hear, they will still be your friend. If they do stop being your friend, then maybe it wasn't the friendship you thought it was.

Why do you care if you piss off the Chef? You're the customer. You're the one spending your hard earned money. They won't throw you out of the restaurant. They won't cause a scene. The worst that will happen is they'll either make you something else or give you back your money. Even if they don't do that, you'll just write it off as a bad experience and never go back again.

What's most important is you don't get the reputation of being a bullshitter. You're not getting away with anything. They know you're not telling them the truth. They're not calling bullshit for the same reasons you're giving them bullshit.

Stop the cycle today. Tell the truth in a way that's not offensive. Tell the truth in a way they can hear you. Telling the truth *will* set you free. Telling the truth will get you to like yourself even more. Liking yourself more is a big step to happiness.

Not telling the truth will create a negative inside yourself and it won't fool the person you're bullshitting. They'll respect you more if you tell them the truth. Respect is another major goal to happiness.

To the people who can't live with themselves unless they say something they don't really believe, I say:

I'm Calling Bullshit!!!

BLOG# 84

Is Food Just For Nourishment?

Food is critical for nourishment. The better your diet, the better you feel. Eating better can help you keep off the unwanted pounds. However, better eating without exercise might not get you the waistline you always wanted. The better you feel and getting to the weight you always wanted, will help you toward your goal of happiness.

The question is, is food only for nourishment? If you're poor, above the poverty level, middle class or higher and live in most countries, food takes on a much larger role in society and the development of your happiness.

Food brings people together. What do we do on most major holidays—we eat! Not just eat anything. We eat the foods of our culture. We eat that food with friends and family. This serves two purposes. It brings people together who might not see each other often and it reminds us of the foods our parents and their parents ate many years ago.

Bringing people together, getting re-involved in their lives, sharing with them what's going on in your life, seeing how they've changed since the last time you saw them, creating new contacts with people you hardly knew and even reminding someone they owe you a hundred bucks (remember, ask for what you want just don't demand it) will make you feel great inside and that's what I call happiness.

Eating the foods of the past might remind you of good times. That first bite might put a video in your brain of a time when you were young and happy. Experiencing past happiness is a great way to enrich today's happiness. Even on holidays like Thanksgiving, most family's mix in a little soul food with their turkey. It's about the food we loved to eat when we were young.

Food should be considered entertainment. Entertainment is not something you do every day. Therefore, many times food is just food (unless you're married to a great chef like my wife). However, on a special day or even a few days a week, you should treat food as entertainment. It might be something naughty like a Whopper at Burger King or a different ethnic dinner you've never eaten before. It doesn't matter. What does matter is it's food you look forward to eating. It's food that feels like you're being entertained. It's food that makes you happy.

Food is only part of the entertainment. At least a few times a month go to a place that not only has great food, but also has an interesting atmosphere. Spend time looking around and enjoy the view. It might be peanut shells on the floor or a fabulous art deco designed room. What's important is you take a step back and take in the interesting and beautiful restaurant you've selected.

Food can also be art. Even if you're single and don't cook, set up the food you eat so it looks good. Treating food as something special (even if it's takeout) will help it taste better and put a smile on your face. Don't say: "it's just food." Don't say: "I don't have time to be creative." Place the takeout on the plate so it looks good to eat. You might be surprised at how interesting you can make the food look.

Being creative with food is another way to enjoy your life. Don't take food for granted. Don't treat it as just nourishment. Try learning how to cook. You don't have to become a chef. Just the fact you tried will make you happy. Don't just slap the food on a plate, eat it in five minutes and sit and watch TV.

What I'm trying to get across is that everything and anything you do in life is an opportunity to enrich your happiness. Going through life unconscious, even about food, is no way to get what you want—which is a happy life. You should take a look at even the little things you do every day and see the happiness opportunity in them.

Look at food as an opportunity, not nourishment. If you're on a strict diet, you can still make the food look interesting. If you're young, you might not understand what I'm talking about, however, I assure you, when you get older you'll realize what an opportunity you passed up by just throwing the food, you ate, down your throat and not appreciating its role in happiness.

When my wife and I go to Vegas there are three kinds of entertainment we love—gambling, shows and food. Those three things make us happy. Soon we're going to Paris and one of the things we're looking forward to is the great food.

Food can make you happy if you pay attention to it. Don't let food be the unforgotten ingredient in your life's goal of happiness.

You deserve <u>all</u> the little things in life that could make you happy.
Food should be one of those things.

BLOG# 85

Sympathy For The Devil

"The idea of heaven and hell came from the Zoroastrian Persian religion In 586 BCE."

I assume some guy who was considered to be a Holy Man (there were no Holy Women back then) came up with the concept. It was a very smart concept. To get people to do the right thing, the holy man created a fantastic place and a horrible place (if you don't know which is Heaven and which is Hell you're probably not from this planet).

Back then people believed in what they couldn't see as long as somebody or something (like a book written by somebody) said it existed. The reward for being good (as described by each individual religion) is a fabulous happy life after death. The punishment for being bad (also described by each individual religion) is a fiery place full of pain and suffering. If it exists, it's where Madoff is going.

I'm not sure I buy into the concept, but if it stops one person from killing another person, I'm all for this Hell thing. The only problem I have with this idea is who decides what's bad enough to get you into Hell and what's good enough to get you into Heaven? It's different in almost every religion and in the brain of every person.

One thing I know, if you believe and follow all the things I've written in my blogs you'll be happy on earth in this life. Therefore, you don't have to worry if Heaven exists because you're already in Heaven.

Now, the guy who can get you to do Hellish things is called the Devil. The internet says the Devil was created by God and therefore, was written in the Bible by the Holy Guys. I believe this idea is bullshit. I believe the Devil was created so people could get away with doing wrong by stating: "the Devil made me do it." I know I'm being cynical and as you can tell, I'm not much into religion, but it is one way of looking at why this ugly guy exists.

By the way, I always wondered why the Devil has never been portrayed as a woman. Oh, I get it; all these writings were written by MEN. I bet a women Devil would be HOT—bad pun EH! On the other hand, there was a time in my life when I thought my first two wives were the Devil.

We all have a little Devil inside us. Even if we're a good person, that little Devil gets us to do bad things. Ever cheat just a little on your taxes? Ever tell a little lie to get out of a jam? Ever not say something when the bartender charged you less than she should have? Ever cheat on a girlfriend? You know I could go on and on. You, better than I, know the little sins you've done. You also know whether those bad doings qualify you to go to Hell.

The point is, your moral compass is ***your*** moral compass. Religions, the Bible, your parents, your friends, etc. are not in charge of your moral compass. If you believe you're a good person, if you believe you can live with the mistakes you've made in your life, if you can look yourself in the mirror and see a good person, then you're not going to Hell.

If you don't believe you're a good person. If you don't believe you can live with the mistakes you've made in your life. If you can't look yourself in the mirror then **YOU'RE ALREADY IN HELL.**

I've made mistakes I would love to take back. I've lied and cheated. However, when I look into the mirror, I see a loving, caring, good and happy person. I like myself. I forgave my indiscretions many years ago,

Am I going to Heaven? I'm really not into that stuff. I'm more focused on what my five senses tell me which is:

"If Heaven is described as a place where you're happy with great friends and loved ones, then I'm already in Heaven!"

BLOG# 86

Today Is The Oldest You've Ever Been And The Youngest You'll Ever Be Again

"Today is the oldest you've ever been and the youngest you'll ever be again"—Oscar De La Hoya.

And you thought he was just a great boxer. My friend Kenny sent me that quote and it has an interesting meaning to me. I know I'm going to get older, but not today. I know today is the youngest I'm ever going to be, but I still see myself as "Kenny from South Philly—still young at heart."

What if you could stop the aging process and freeze your age at any stage of your life? Would you freeze it at today's age? Would you freeze it at an age when you were much, much younger? Would you freeze it ten years ago or would you freeze it ten years from now?

Before you answer quickly, think about it. Usually the first thing in your mind would be to freeze it at a younger age than today. Isn't younger better? Most likely your physical health was better than today. However, younger might not be the right answer.

Most 13 year old kids would want to freeze their age at 20. Most 60 year old people would want to freeze their age at least twenty years younger. However, if you really consider what was happening in your life, at that time, and what you had to deal with years later, you might change your mind.

"At 13, I was poor but I didn't know it—I was having fun" (from my first book "Never Buy A Hat If Your Feet Are Cold"). However, I wanted to be older. At 20, I could drive a car, have sex (yes I even thought about sex at thirteen), make money, buy more things and be an astronaut.

Even though thirteen was a blast, I wouldn't want to freeze my age at 13.

When I was 20, I got married (can you spell SEX), drove a car, had an interesting job and made more money than my father. I wasn't an astronaut, but I was a fantastic computer programmer and almost got a job with NASA.

However, just two years later, I had two screaming kids and a screaming wife. The company I worked for made me a manager of five employees. I went from a software creator to a parent. All my employees were older than I and weren't happy I was promoted over them. This was the first time in my life where stress made life less fun.

Even though I would never get older than 20, the years going by didn't make me happy and therefore, I wouldn't want to freeze my age when I was 20.

At 30, my life wasn't so hot. I was learning and growing in a business I loved, but the stress of the job and the realization that my marriage was not working and divorce was in the future was UGH! Also, the negative impact divorce had on my kids was terrible and the loss of friends made my 30's not my best of times.

Although 30 is a great age from a physical point of view, it doesn't mean it will be a great mental and emotional time. In my case, it wasn't, so I wouldn't want to freeze my age when I was 30.

At 40 I was in a yin and yang time of my life. I was going through yet another divorce. I had no money (paying two alimony and two child support payments plus the loss of my house). My oldest son divorced me. I was having serious back and neck problems that required surgery. My mental outlook sucked and I needed help. However, my career was booming, I met the best thing in my life—my wife and we were able to travel internationally.

40's yin was great, but I still wouldn't want to go through that yang again. Sooo, I wouldn't want to freeze my age when I was 40.

At 50 things were getting better. I had a wife who anyone would kill to have (just an expression), I had the opportunity to run a software company in Vancouver. I got to live in Amsterdam for a year. The things I learned from my therapist were taking hold and my mental outlook was going in the right direction. However, my body sucked and my work was extremely stressful.

Even though there were more good things than bad things going on at 50, I just can't say I would want to freeze my age when I was 50.

Now I'm in my 60's. I'm retired. I have very little stress. I still have the best wife in the world. I have great and interesting friends. My son and daughter-in law are the best and my two grandchildren are fantastic. My mental outlook is full of positive energy. I have freedom of choice. I know things about my physical and mental situation and what to do to avoid any more problems. I'm more confident. I'm less insecure. I like myself more. I give positive energy out to the universe and it's giving it back to me.

These are the best years of my life! Therefore, I want to freeze my age as of today. What about you? Are these the best years of your life? Do you need to go back in time or do you believe tomorrow will be much better?

Think about it! Write it down. You might be surprised at what you come up with.

Always remember, happiness is your goal. You can't freeze your age so you better make today and the years ahead the best of your life.

BLOG# 87

Why Get Up

Ever feel so down you ask yourself why get up? Ever feel the whole world has gone so crazy you might as well stay in bed? Ever feel so nervous about what your day is going to be like you just prefer to stay in bed rather than face the day? Ever feel like your marriage or friendship is so over you just want to pull the covers over your head and sleep all day? I have and I'm sure many things have happened in your life that has made you feel like ***why get up***.

The question is what did you do during those days, weeks, months or years? Some people fight through it while some people just pull the covers over their head. I'm the lower my head and blast through it type of person.

Usually when you've gone through multiple situations it gets easier each additional time. The first time is hell. Loss of a boyfriend, loss of a loved one, financial disaster, etc. is really tough the first time and it's normal to feel like staying in bed and never getting up.

Some people will do anything to avoid getting hurt or taking a risk that might lead to a problem. Those people are thinking to themselves: "I don't want anything bad happening to me so ***why get up***?

That's the wrong way to create a happy life. Take it from me, each major loss gets easier to overcome if you overcame the first one. The reason is simple, the more you do anything the easier and the better you get at doing it. For example, if your boyfriend left you for another girl, and you were able to get over it, the next time it happens still feels like shit, but you realize you got over the first one and now believe you'll get over this one.

Believe it or not, by getting over really bad situations builds confidence in you. Just like in baseball, the more hits you get the better you become at hitting. Your confidence keeps getting better the more hits you get.

Never going through a really bad time in your life sounds like something everybody wishes would happen. I don't agree. The easier life is for you the less life you get. The harder life is for you the more you appreciate getting through the hard times.

The challenge is to pat yourself on the back for being able to overcome difficulties without putting up barriers. Barriers are not a good solution. Taking drugs is not a good solution. Pulling the covers over your head is not a good solution. The best solution is to feel good about losing someone who didn't love you in the first place and get out of bed and find one who will.

As a true friend, you have an obligation to do everything you can to help your friends to get back in the trenches and fight another day. Your day might be coming and you would want them to do the same for you.

Sooo, cherish the times when you were able to overcome the problems in your life or future problems that might arise. These problems are character building. These problems are confidence building. These problems are part of life.

Life without problems to overcome will not make you happier. If you don't believe me, get a lobotomy. At least that way you won't give a shit if problems do arise.

The answer to ***"why get up"*** is:

The more you appreciate yourself for the things you've overcome, the better your life will get.
You deserve a better life.

BLOG# 88

What A Ride

"Life shouldn't be a journey to the grave with the intention of arriving safely in an attractive and well preserved body, but rather to skid in sideways, body thoroughly used up, totally worn out and screaming what a ride!"

I was watching Real Sports on HBO and the first segment was about a professional football player who after spending eight years as a pro retired from football. Most fans don't know his name, but they do remember his blocked punt that won a game for the New Orleans Saints football team after the Katrina disaster. That block punt made the people of New Orleans feel they could overcome this disaster and rebuild their great city.

Steve Gleason is his name. He not only was a very good football player, he's an avid sports fan, loves to fish, loves to travel, loves to motor boat and loves the crap out of life. What I didn't say is that two years after he retired (he's 33), he contracted ALS.

For those of you who don't know about ALS, it's a horrible disease that attacks the muscles of your body while it leaves your brain intact. Therefore, you know what's happening to you as your body becomes a vegetable and eventually dies because your lungs stop working.

Most people just give up when they get ALS—not Steve. Yes, he started out angry and frustrated. However, when he realized what was ahead of him, he started planning how he could make a life for himself as long as life would have him.

In the segment, Steve is still fishing, boat riding and traveling—obviously with the help of others. His wife says she believes the reason Steve is still getting a lot out of life is because, from the early stage of his disease, he asked for help. Instead of being depressed about his situation, he learned what he could accomplish and let the people who cared for him help make it happen. He realized being macho about it wouldn't work.

Steve quoted: "I don't focus on what my body can't do; I focus on what my body can do." He knows he soon won't be able to write or type on a computer. Therefore, he's learning how to use a special computer that allows him to type on his computer using only his eyes.

From the outset of the disease Steve wanted to leave something behind for his infant son (yes, he was able to have a child). He started to video tape segments where he told his son about his disease, how much he still loved life and how much he loved his son and his wife. It was heart-breaking to watch some of his videos because his voice kept getting worse as the weeks and months progressed.

Today, Steve has a great deal of difficulty communicating, but you can still see how smart and articulate he is. He's keeps up with what is going on in the world and can discuss events as good as people who don't have his handicap.

The bottom line is, Steve Gleason believes:

"Life shouldn't be a journey to the grave with the intention of arriving safely in an attractive and well preserved body, but rather to skid in sideways, body thoroughly used up, totally worn out and screaming what a ride!"

What about you? Are you playing it too safe? Is your goal to just get through life as unscathed as possible? Are you trying to enjoy all the moments you have left?

Are you willing to take risks, love again even though you were hurt, ask for a better job even though you might get fired, learn new things, make new friends, forgive yourself for all the mistakes you've made in your life, love yourself for all the accomplishments you've done in your life and can't wait to attack the future challenges ahead of you?

I'm a lifer. I watched my Father and Mother get very little out of life. They played it safe and didn't live life like the saying above. I decided early on to take on my life journey face first. I decided to get the most of what my life has to offer and when it does end:

Scream At The Top Of My Lungs:
"What A Ride."

BLOG# 89

Death

If you're close to 50 or older you probably know many of the world's icons who have passed away in the last few years. Sadly, you probably have a few friends and family who have died. My Mom, Dad and Sister are all dead. Some of the movie, music, theater and paint artists I grew up with have died. Some of the most brilliant minds are dead. Neil Armstrong died the other day.

What this tells me is I'm *almost* surely going to die. I'm leaving a little hope out there because who knows what science might come up with. Remember, drug and healthcare companies really don't want people to die because the only people who make money on dead people are the undertakers and the mortuaries.

The thing is, I'm going to live until November 11, 2038 (I'll be 94). That means many of the people I know probably won't make it that long. My heart will ache when they die. However, I'm sorry to be so crass, but better them than I. As I said in my previous blog, I'm going to ride this body until it doesn't work anymore. On November 11, 2038 I'll be screaming "What A Ride."

The death of the people I know has got me thinking. Do I fear death? The answer for me is NO! I do fear losing my mind. My brain is my strength. Using my brain makes me happy. As long as my brain is functioning I can make a great life for myself. My limbs are just the bumpers. My brain is the engine. My brain can still live a good life even if all my bumpers fall off.

Do I fear the people I know might die before me? Again, sorry to be crass, but NO! What happens to them isn't in my control. What happens to them isn't my fault. I won't stop trying to get the most happiness I deserve out of life if they all die. I wish them well and want them to be with me as long as possible, but what's it my business if they kick-off.

Will I take the best care of myself I can to make sure I make it to 2038—ABSOLUTELY! Drugs and vitamins are my friends. Exercise makes me happy. However, I like my booze and I love a great hamburger. It makes me happy to do a few things that might risk my iffy back and neck (like dancing my ass off). On the other hand, I'm not going down a ski slope, drive 100 MPH in a 50

MPH zone, jump out of anything or doing the Limbo (if you don't know what the Limbo is, you're too young to think about death—read my other blogs).

The death of the people I know has made me realize a few other things. Appreciate and love everyone you know. Don't wait until they die to say nice things about them. Say those things NOW! What I mean by NOW is NOW—like today. Think about what you want to say and say it the second they're in your presence. Enjoy their company as if you know they're going to die sometime soon. Tell them what's going on inside you. Share your hopes, dreams and fears with them. The more you expose yourself, the more they might expose themselves.

Even though I'm going to live until November 11, 2038, I *am* going to die. Sooo, these have to be the best years of my life. I have to find happiness in everything I do. I don't have the luxury of taking anything for granted. I have to step back and appreciate my surroundings. I have to appreciate every detail of my life. I have to appreciate living.

What about YOU? Do these icons, your friends or family members dying make you depressed? Do you fear your mortality? Would you prefer to *not* outlive your kids, spouse, etc.? It's normal to say yes to those feelings. The question is, what are you going to do about it?

Worrying about death doesn't have to be a bad thing as long as you're using that fear to get closer to your friends and family, working to get all the happiness you deserve, doing what you can to live longer and:

Appreciating the wonders of your life NOW!!

BLOG# 90

It's A Look

"I would rather look good than feel good"
Ricardo Montalbán

(Born November 25, 1920-Died January 14, 2009) was a Mexican radio, television, theater and film actor. He had a career spanning seven decades (motion pictures from 1943 to 2006) and many notable roles. During the mid-1970s, Montalbán was notable as the spokesman in automobile advertisements for the Chrysler Cordoba, in which he famously extolled the "soft Corinthian leather" used for its interior. He became famous as Mr. Roarke, the main star in the television series Fantasy Island. He played in the 1982 film Star Trek II: The Wrath of Khan. He won an Emmy Award in 1978 for his role in the miniseries How the West Was Won[2] and a Lifetime Achievement Award from the Screen Actors Guild in 1993. Into his 80s, he continued to perform, often providing voices for animated

films and commercials, and appearing in several Spy Kids films as "Grandfather Valentin".

I'm sure he was joking, but his, in front of the camera; persona would make you believe he was telling the truth. He always looked fantastic even when he was eighty. He dressed to the hilt. His hair was always perfect and his accent just made his physical being look even better.

What's really interesting is, I have come across people (men and women) who would make the same statement. How they look is critical to their self-worth and their self being.

What I've also found in my many years of people watching is more than 75 percent of people have a look. I assume it must be how they see themselves. Some look like they're still living in the 50's. Some look like they started in the 70's movie "Disco Fever." Some have purple hair. Some wear their pants so low you can see the crack in their ass.

Starting today, do some people watching! It's a lot of fun. When my wife points someone out to me I always say to her "It's a look." What I mean by that is even if I believe they look ridiculous it's their look. It's how they want the outside world to see them. Judging them is wrong. Enjoying their personal statement is right.

Steve Jobs had a look—tee shirt, jeans and a sports jacket. Johnny Cash had a look—black. Phyllis Diller had a look—wild. Hitler had a look—and it wasn't pretty. I could go on and on, but you get the idea. Take a step back and enjoy their look—its fun.

Judging other peoples' looks is wrong. What I mean by that is seeing someone and saying: "look at him—he must be gay (not that there is anything wrong with that)." "Look at the way she's dressed—she must be a hooker." Judging without even knowing a person is wrong, wrong, wrong.

I love bright colors. I wear red sneakers. I have a pair of blue and brown glasses and a pair of red and black glasses. Does that mean I'm gay? Not that there's anything wrong with that, but my wife would disagree.

My wife's look is always a beautiful lady. Even in jeans, she makes sure she looks beautiful. My look is anything that makes her happy. I don't really care so I let her pick out my clothes. I do want to look good and she helps me look great. My friend Kenny didn't have a look until he let his hair grow very long. Now that's his look. We hate it, but it's *his* look.

I do have a problem with people who will do major things to their body to get a look. Going from a 34 bust to a 38 bust via plastic surgery is a look, but at what price. It's not just the money. You'll have a bad back the rest of your life and when you get old those balloons will really look terrible. Getting surgery so you look better in clothes, doesn't work for me. How about finding clothes that make you look good just the way you are.

Doing cosmetic surgery so you keep looking younger is something I can live with as long as you don't get addicted to it. You all have seen people who did too much and now they don't look natural. I look at cosmetic surgery this way:

- Will the surgery make me sexier to my wife?
- Will my friends love me more if I have the surgery?
- Will I hit the lottery if I have surgery?
- Will I write or play the guitar better if I have surgery?
- Will I like myself better if I have the surgery?
- Can I stand seeing that old guy in the mirror?

In my case the answer to all but the last one is NO! The last one "can I stand seeing that old guy in the mirror" is yes. The reason is, when I look in the mirror I see my eyes. What my eyes look like is "Kenny from South Philly"—young at heart and full of life. Therefore, there isn't any cosmetic surgery in my future.

What's your look? If you don't have one, think about getting one. Don't do it for "them," do it for you. Don't think about how *they* will see and judge you—think about how *you* want them to see you. It's your look and nobody can take it away from you. If they don't like it—who gives a shit?

Please remember, beauty is in the mind of the beholder. See beauty in as many things as you can. If someone you know completely changes his look and your first reaction is you don't approve, slap yourself upside your head and say:

It's A Look"

BLOG# 91

You Are What You Were Given And What You Decide To Be

***"You Are What You Were Given And What You Decide To Be"* Kenny Felderstein**

California people are lazy summer hummers. Minnesota people are the salt of the earth. New York people are loud and abrasive. People in the deep south of America are uneducated and stupid. People in New England are rich and stuck-up.

People in Mexico are lazy and stupid. People in Japan are uptight. People in North Korea are behind the times. People in England don't smile and are too formal. People in Russia are gangsters and nasty. People in France are abrupt and won't talk to you unless you speak French. People in Italy are lazy, non-business like and never get anything done. Women in Spain and some Latin

American countries love sex. People in Holland are big and friendly. Women in Sweden are big, blond and beautiful.

How many of the statements above are true? From my US and International experience the women in Sweden *are* big, blond and beautiful and the people in Holland *are* big and friendly. All the other statements are stereotypes.

"You Are What You Were Given." People in California, Mexico and Italy aren't lazy, it's just the pace is slower than places like New York City. People whose parents and their parents grew up in a place where things got done when they got done will most likely grow up getting things done when they get done. People whose parents and their parents grew up a place where life was slower, a place where options were limited, a place where money, ego and power were not the driving forces in their lives, these people will probably live the way their parents lived *unless* "**What You Decide To Be"** is something different.

The statement, New York people are loud and abrasive is both true and not true. **"You Are What You Were Given."** New York City is small (based upon the number of people), loud (because of the traffic) and congested. People have to dance around many, many people just to get where they're going. You get frustrated because everyone is in a hurry. You get desensitized to the people around you because someone will always be in your way.

If you and your parents grew up in New York City or the other New York-like congested cities, you probably are loud and abrasive *unless* **"What You Decide To Be"** is something different.

If you grew up in the other cities of New York State, life was very different. I lived one year one month and four hours in Rochester, New York (I guess I didn't like the weather). I came from congested Philadelphia. I was loud and sometimes abrasive. That attitude didn't work in Rochester. I decided to be something different.

Women in Spain and some Latin American countries love sex—NOT! Just because they live in a warm climate and wear short, tight, colorful and sexy skirts doesn't make them sex maniacs. I'm not saying they don't like sex (how would I know—right sweetheart), but I'm sure their sexual habits are no different than women in other countries.

"You Are What You Were Given." If your DNA and your upbringing pointed to being more sexual, then you probably like sex more than someone with different DNA and a different upbringing. However, if **"What You Decide To Be"** is someone who gives sexual favors to get money, security or power, you're probably a hooker or someone who's married to a Sugar Daddy.

People in France are abrupt and won't talk to you unless you speak French—flat out Bullshit!! I just came from France and the people were so nice. I speak almost no French and yet I was able to do everything I wanted to do in Paris and the rest of France because the people were patient with me and tried to help.

"You Are What You Were Given." If you grew up with family who treated foreigners with disrespect you probably would treat others with disrespect *unless* **"What You Decide To Be"** is someone who loves life and gives respect to all the people they ever met in their lives. The worldlier you become and the more people you meet from different countries and cultures, the better chance you have to love and respect all the people in your life.

You know I could go on and on, but I won't because I believe you get my point. If not, here it is:

We all have been given a specific DNA. We all have been brought up in a specific environment. That's why **"You Are What You Were Given."** We all could just live the way our parents brought us up or the way our DNA makes us. If you can have a happy and positive energy life with those two things—fabulous don't change a thing.

However, if life is not a bowl of cherries for you or if what you were *given* isn't working for you, then you have to believe you have the power to create:

"What You Decide To Be."

BLOG# 92

Resolutions

It's the start of the Jewish New Year. Like other New Years, we ate until our underwear no longer fit. What is different about the Jewish New Year and the New Year that starts at the beginning of the calendar year is that Jews don't make resolutions because of the Jewish New Year.

Resolutions are both a good thing and a not so good thing. If you have to wait for New Years to make a resolution, you're not real serious about the resolution in the first place. For example, if you say: "my New Year's resolution is to stop smoking." I believe your odds of accomplishing the resolution is less than twenty percent. If you want to stop smoking, take the steps to do so now. This might be the hardest thing you've ever accomplished so don't believe waiting for New Year will make it easier.

The good part of making resolutions is you have an idea of what you have to improve in your life. The goal of your resolutions should be ones that will make you happier. Improving your health is a great resolution. Stop being angry at someone who has done you wrong is a great resolution. Getting rid of the things and/or the people in your life that have made you unhappy is a great resolution. Deciding to get more out of life is a great resolution.

Getting a dog, buying a car, getting a new home, paying your bills on time, saving money, going out more, seeing your children, etc. etc. are not resolutions. These are the everyday things you should be doing as a way of life.

Getting revenge is a bad resolution. Doing something you really don't want to do, but it will make you more money, is a bad resolution. Buying a car or house that you really can't afford is a bad resolution. Leaving the job you love and are great at for a promotion to one that has more stress, less fun, but has more money and more power, is a bad resolution. Stop taking risks is a bad resolution.

I don't make resolutions. They can be restricting. They can make me unhappy if they don't happen. My goal is to get the most out of the life that is available to me. I don't want to make a resolution I have to do because one day later my priorities might change. I don't want to make a resolution that requires the outside world to reach my goal. I don't want to make a resolution where things I can't control could make me unhappy.

I want to live life doing the things that make me happy. I want to appreciate the things I have accomplished. I want to pat myself on the back for the problems I've overcome. I want to believe I have control of my happiness.

I want to love myself unconditionally. Now that's a fabulous resolution!

BLOG# 93

If You Want To Do Something, Find A Way If You Don't Want To Do Something, Find An Excuse

I'm not sure where I read that statement, but I somewhat agree with the first statement and disagree with the second. Let's take them apart:

"If you want to do something, find a way."

I can agree with that statement as long as the "something" is doable. I want to be a National Football League Quarterback, but I don't have the skills, the physical attributes or the experience to find a way.

I wanted to retire at sixty two so I had to find a way. My wife and I saved our money. We didn't buy cars, houses or stuff we couldn't afford. We stayed in the same home for over 20 years. We agreed to tighten our belt and spend less after I retired. That's what I call finding a way.

If I wanted to be a Rocket Scientist, I could have found a way. I have the brains. I spent my career in computers. What I don't have is the knowledge and the experience. Knowledge comes from reading, education, and experience. I could spend my available hours reading and going to school. I could take a low paying job getting coffee for a real Rocket Scientist. Picking his brain, as I learn, could get me a little higher job in the field. Years later I would get an even higher job and after many years I would be a Rocket Scientist.

You see, there is a difference in finding a way to do something and wanting to do something. I believe I could be a Rocket Scientist, but I don't want it enough to spend the years I have left in my life getting there. Also, I'm loving retirement, my guitar, the people I mentor, my wife, my dog, my time with my friends, my gym and my blogging.

If you decide you want to do something, you will find a way if:

- You have the skills.
- You have the mental capacity.

- You have the physical attributes necessary to make it happen.

- Most importantly, you have the strong desire to get what you want because getting it will improve your life, make you happier and put positive energy into your life.

"If you don't want to do something, find an excuse."

I really don't agree with that statement. My statement would be: ***"If you don't want to do something, don't do it."*** If you really don't want to take your grandchildren for the weekend, don't do it. That's right; tell your son or daughter you don't want to do it. If they really want to have some private time without their kids, they **"will find a way."** Also, they will be upset because you said no, but they'll still love you.

Making up some bullshit excuse is the wrong course. "We have other plans that weekend" won't work. What if they say: "that's OK dad, we can do it the next weekend." Now you're trapped. Are you going to say to them you also have plans for the following weekend? They're not stupid. It will hurt them more if you give them an excuse they know is bullshit rather than telling them you just don't want to do it. Don't cop out. Just tell them the truth.

If you don't want to lend money to a friend or family member, don't do it. If they get pissed off at you because you said no, so be it. A true friend will understand. A true friend won't ask for money because they know it might negatively impact their relationship with you.

Making up excuses to soften the blow is chickening out. Excuses like: "I'd have to ask my wife, but I'm sure she won't go for it, "I'll try to get the money—call me next week," "Things are tight right now—maybe I can help you a month from now." These excuses will all be thought of as dishonest excuses.

Don't cop out. Just tell them the truth which is you're not going to give them the money because you worked hard to get it and you know lending money is the best way to screw up a friendship.

People use excuses because they fear if they just say no, they won't be liked. If you think you're doing so because you don't want to hurt the other person's feelings, that's bullshit, you know it and it doesn't work. They'll know you're just making up an excuse. Real people want the truth. Real friends will respect you more if you tell them the truth.

Making up excuses so you won't feel guilty is not a way to run your life. You're not guilty. You're not doing anything wrong. You know who you are and like yourself just the way you are. Therefore, if they don't like you telling them your real feelings, they're not the people you want in your life.

Lastly, never make excuses to yourself. What I mean by that is, if you and others feel you should take that promotion, but you really don't want the stress, don't make up some internal bullshit excuse to yourself. "I can't take it now because I'll disappoint my current manager." "I can't leave this project just now, I'm sure I'll get another chance later." "The people who work with me now will have to work harder if I leave." These are just bad internal excuses for something you really don't want to do.

Don't cop out. Tell yourself, your spouse and your family, I love my current job and I don't want the stress of the new job even if it gives us more money.

Please believe me, any decision you make for your happiness is a great decision. Bullshit excuses are always bad decisions.

BLOG# 94

Beauty *IS* Only Skin Deep

The October 1973 oil crisis started when the members of Organization of Arab Petroleum Exporting Countries or OAPEC proclaimed an oil embargo. This was in response to the U.S. decision to re-supply the Israeli military during the Yom Kippur war. It lasted until March 1974.

In Pennsylvania you could only get five dollars' worth of gas every other day. One way of beating the system was to get on the national turnpike. There you could ride the turnpike and stop at every station to fill up. The problem was you had to use gas to get to the turnpike and pay the turnpike toll. If you had a job and needed your car to get to work, money was not an issue.

Even after it was over, people were saying this crisis was going to happen again and again. General Motors saw an opportunity to make money by building diesel engine cars. Mercedes had been building diesel cars for many, many years before the crisis.

When I came to California in 1976, my first wife and I decided to get a diesel car because they got more miles per gallon and if gas became limited again, diesel was always available.

Not knowing what I know now, prestige was important to both my wife and me. I decided to get a low end Mercedes diesel. I went to the Orange County Mercedes dealer and took the car for a test ride. The car was very under powered and struggled to get up a steep hill.

My wife and I agreed it wasn't worth the money to buy a low powered Mercedes. General Motors had just come out with a Cadillac Eldorado Biarritz diesel. It was gorgeous and that was important to both of us. The test drive went great. The car had lots of power and was priced the same as the Mercedes. We bought it on the spot.

Three month after my purchase I was driving on the freeway and the car stopped. It didn't just come to a slow stop—it came to a giant thud stop. The dealer had to replace the engine because it froze up. A few months later I was driving around town and guess what, the engine froze up again. I was just happy it didn't happen on the freeway.

The dealer's service manager told me this was happening to other Cadillac diesel cars. He explained this was happening because diesel fuel was dirty and had much more moisture than gas cars. Big trucks and, by the way, the Mercedes had and have water separators connected to the fuel line to filter out the dirt and water. General Motors didn't build their diesel cars with a water separator. Their position was I should get diesel from a filling station that had cleaner diesel.

After replacing another engine, I realized the problem didn't occur when I got diesel fuel from a station close to my home. This was good except I was paranoid to get fuel from anywhere else. I could live with that because the car was so beautiful.

Around the seventh or eighth month I was on the freeway and again the car made an sound I hadn't heard before and came to a stop. When Triple A (AAA) came out and looked under the hood they said my fan belt had come off. They got me to the dealer—again.

The service manager told me Cadillac had taken the standard gas engine and made it into a diesel. The good news was the engine was very powerful. The bad news was a diesel engine vibrates three times as much as a gas engine which was the cause of the fan belt flying off.

He gave me three extra belts and a wrench. He then showed me how to put on the belt should it come off again. Even though I was scared to drive on the freeway, I could live with this problem because the car was so beautiful.

Ten months into this disaster the car was running fine except for the two new belts I had to put on. Then, while driving, I heard a loud rattling sound coming from the engine area. I immediately went to the dealer. The service manager, who was as frustrated as I, said the reason this was happening was because a diesel engine runs much hotter than a gas engine and the noise I was hearing was the pan under the engine to protect the drive train from the heat.

The pan was just fine; however the bolts holding the pan in place had melted from the engine heat which caused the pan to rattle. He said the pan would not cause a problem, but if I wanted to stop the rattling I needed to leave the car for two days. I couldn't leave it because I had a business meeting at an expensive restaurant in downtown Los Angeles.

So there I am, holding my breath while driving on the freeway with a car whose engine might freeze, a fan belt that might fly off and a rattling noise that could be heard from a hundred feet away. I was so embarrassed giving my keys to the valet while he was asking if my beautiful Cadillac Eldorado Biarritz diesel was working OK. I told him the rattling noise was not a problem; however I showed him where I put the fan belts in case they were needed.

The day my one year warranty was over I traded in my beautiful car for an ugly, boxy Volvo 240 that had the best reliability rating by Consumer Reports. I was so happy the Volvo dealer took my beautiful Cadillac Eldorado Biarritz diesel. I hugged him (which he thought was strange).

BTW, I had the Volvo for five years and it never had a problem. It was ugly, but I smiled every time I got on the freeway. Two years after I traded in my Cadillac, General Motors stopped producing diesel cars for the American market.

I shouldn't have to give you the moral to this story, but I will. Beauty IS only skin deep. Shiny objects can confuse you. Beautiful design doesn't mean great craftsmanship. A pretty face doesn't mean a good heart and soul.

Make sure you look under the hood before you buy, make friends or marry. Don't dive into anything because of a beautiful facade.

It's what's inside that will make you happy.

BLOG# 95

What Are *They* Afraid Of?

What are *they* afraid of? Well, first, who are *they*? "They" are ordinary people, rich and poor, religious and not, people of the world, all colors, all faiths, even a Vice President candidate named Paul Ryan.

Are *they* afraid that everyone will become gay and the human race will eventually end because nobody will have babies? Any intelligent person knows that won't ever happen. The worst case is, if it did happen, gay guys would make babies with gay women. There are gay women married and having babies. Sooo, if anyone is afraid that the human race will stop to exist, they need a mental health specialist.

Are *they* afraid gay people will make them and their children gay? I don't know of one gay organization dedicated to doing so. There are organizations that want to bring down the government. There are organizations that want to eliminate all people who are not white. There are organizations that want to destroy the Jews, the Muslims and the gays. However, I don't know of any gay organizations or groups of gay people that want everyone else to be gay.

Are *they* afraid that gay people will rape and plunder them? There are approximately 208,000 rapes a year. Much—much less than 1% are caused by a gay person. There are over a million crimes each year. Gays represent a very tiny percentage. However, crimes against gays are much higher than the number of crimes perpetrated by gays.

Are *they* afraid that God will strike them down if they accept and support gays and gay marriage? The Church says yes because the Bible tells them so. If you believe the Bible is the message from God, then please think about how it was written. It didn't show up in book form out of the blue. It wasn't etched in stone. Holy people received a message from God and wrote it down.

Holy people are wonderful, but they *are* human. Maybe they got the message wrong. Maybe their fathers and mothers were afraid of gay people. Maybe gays having sex disgusted them. The one thing I do know is these holy people were not gay. If they were, maybe, just maybe, the message from God would have been written differently.

Are *they* afraid that every guy will start wearing leather or dress up in woman's clothing and wear make-up? OK, work with me here, I'm just trying my best to figure out what the hell they're afraid of. You do know that heterosexual men's cosmetic face and skin products are a fast growing market.

I know some of the gay communities look different. Some of the women look like men and some of the men look like women. However, is that something to be afraid of? I know thinking about two men having sex is not something I want to visualize. However, two women having sex, now that's a different story.

The facts are gay people are just like us. They work just like us. They worry about finances just like us. They fall in love just like us. They have gay and not gay friendships just like many of us. They have bad days and good days just like us. They adopt children just like us. They love their children just like us. They try their best to make a happy life for their children just like us. Most of all, just like us, they want to have a happy life.

Do you really believe if they marry, your life will be worse? Do you really believe if they marry, the Church will go under? Do you really believe if they marry, your children and their children will grow up in a demon world? Do you really believe if they marry the United

States and the rest of the world will fall apart? Come on, you know the answer to these questions is NO!

Sooo, what the hell are *they* afraid of. I really don't know and I'm not sure *they* know. I have never heard anyone give me a specific reason as to why being gay is wrong. Saying the Bible says so, is leaving all your decisions to a book. Saying it's just not right, is not an intelligent answer. Saying that's the way I was brought up, is giving control of your life to your parents. Saying it disgusts me, is saying you have no insight as to how you feel about things.

Probably many of my readers have no problem with gay people, but some know people who do. Probably some of my readers have no problem with gay marriage, however those who do, please ask yourself: "what am I afraid of?" "What's the worst that can happen?" "Will anybody who loves me stop loving me?" Will my journey to happiness crumble?"

Being afraid of gays, Muslims, etc. etc. is no way to live your life. Unless you have a really good reason, don't let fears of anybody make you unhappy!

Loving Unconditionally Is An Important Way To Live A Life Of Happiness.

BLOG# 96

Is It Fate Or Destiny Or Does Shit Just Happen?

"Although the words are used interchangeably in many cases, fate and destiny can be distinguished. Traditional usage defines fate as a power or agency that predetermines and orders the course of events. Fate defines events as ordered or "inevitable" and unavoidable. Classical and European mythology features three goddesses dispensing fate, known as Moirai in Greek mythology, as Parcae in Roman mythology, and as Norns in Norse mythology. They determine the events of the world through the mystic spinning of threads that represent individual human fates.

Destiny is used with regard to the finality of events as they have worked themselves out; and that same sense of Destination, projected into the future to become

the flow of events as they will work themselves out. In other words, fate relates to events of the future and present of an individual and in cases in literature unalterable, whereas destiny relates to the probable future. Fate implies no choice, but with destiny the entity is participating in achieving an outcome that is directly related to itself. Participation happens willfully."

How many of you believe when shit happens it's just fate? How many of you believe when shit happens it's just destiny? How many of you believe when shit happens it's just shit happening? I believe shit just happens.

I really don't believe in fate. Fate assumes something is controlling what happens and how it turns out. Fate assumes I have no control over what happens or its outcome because the thing that's making it happen is not of this world.

I also don't believe in destiny.

"Fate implies no choice, but with destiny the entity is participating in achieving an outcome that is directly related to itself. Participation happens willfully."

Look, I've been preaching to you that you're in control of your happiness. I agree with that because you can make choices to be happy or sad. You might not like the choices, but you can make them. Poor people can be happy. Money can help, but it's not necessary. A paraplegic can be happy. Nobody wants that to happen to themselves or anybody else, but if it does, that person *can* choose to find happiness or give up and be miserable with the life they have left.

However, saying you have control of your destiny is bullshit. You can control what you do, but you can't control what "it" does. "It" is the outside human world and Mother Nature. You can't control the people you know. You can't control terrorism, bigotry, arson or some nut blowing something up. You definitely can't control Mother Nature.

Sooo, for these reasons, I believe shit just happens. Once you accept that as fact your life will get better. Believing in fate will never make you happy because you'll have given up ***all*** control. Believing in destiny will frustrate you because the things you can't control will find a way to make you unhappy.

Accepting that shit just happens enables you to think about what you're going to do about it and then take action. Somebody smashed my car. Was it fate? Was it destiny? No, it was just some asshole talking on his cell phone. Now that you've accepted that there are assholes in this world and shit just happens, what are you going to do about the smashed car? You're going to get it fixed!!

It's wrong to live your life counting on fate or destiny. It's wrong to live your life blaming fate or destiny.

"It's right to enjoy living in a chaotic world where you never know when shit will just happen because you can then decide how you want to react to the chaos."

BLOG# 97

Disappoint Everyone, Disappoint Anyone, But Never Disappoint Yourself

Sometimes people who write TV shows say something profound. It doesn't happen often, but when it does it can really hit a home run. I wish I knew which author wrote:

"Disappoint Everyone, Disappoint Anyone, But Never Disappoint Yourself."

If I did, I would assume he or she has written other profound sayings. I'm going to tell you what this saying means to me. However, you should think long and hard about what it means to you.

Let's start at the end; ***"Never Disappoint Yourself."*** Do you feel disappointed? Did you make decisions in your life that made you feel disappointed with yourself? Were you ever in a friendship or relationship that wound up disappointing you? Did you avoid making a tough decision and feel disappointed in your lack of action? Do you feel life will find a way to disappoint you? When you get disappointed do you stop liking yourself? When you get disappointed do you feel not good enough? Do you feel disappointed all the time?

If the answer is "yes" to any or all of the above, you're not on a good path to happiness. To get back on path, you have three choices.

1. Avoid, at all costs, doing anything that might lead to you being disappointed.

2. Do something that might disappoint "them" but will not disappoint you.

3. Stop being disappointed.

Number one is not the right answer and won't work. Avoiding life so you don't disappoint yourself is not living life. Living life to the fullest is the right path to happiness. As I've been telling you, always ask yourself "what's the worst that can happen? Even if the worst happens I believe I will recover." An interesting life is more interesting when you've had disappointments and lived through them. Don't cheat yourself out of a happy life because you fear being disappointed. Remember:

"If you make more right decisions than wrong decisions that's great, but NO decision IS a wrong decision." By Kenny Felderstein

Number two will work, but might have some consequences. You should always put yourself in first position. You should always love yourself just a little more than anyone or anything else. Making a major change, making a major decision, putting yourself ahead of everyone else, might disappoint friends, family, children, church, team, bosses, co-workers, but if you're doing so for your happiness it shouldn't disappoint you.

You should never feel disappointed if you've disappointed others because you want a better life. Let the others deal with "their" disappointment. The people who care and love you will get over their disappointment. If you disappointed others because you tried something new and failed don't let it disappoint you. You'll try again and succeed or you'll realize you're over your head on this action and will try something you're more capable of doing right. Never be disappointed because you tried and failed. Feel great about yourself because you tried in the first place.

If you disappointed others because you just didn't give a shit, you're not a good person, you're not a happy person and you don't give positive energy out to the Universe.

People like that don't get disappointed by anything "they" do because they don't have a love for life.

Number three is the best choice. If you get disappointed, get over it quickly. It's not helping your happiness meter by staying disappointed. Long term disappointment leads to depression. Long term disappointment leads to poor health. Long term disappointment leads to not feeling good about yourself. Long term disappointment leads to more disappointment.

Whatever you did that made you disappointed, is not life threatening. Whatever you did that made you disappointed, will go away sooner the less you focus on it. Whatever you did that made you disappointed can be corrected. Whatever you did that made you disappointed is just a moment in time.

You have the power to be happy. You have the power to make a better life for yourself. You have the power to not be disappointed at any action you take that might lead to your happiness.

BLOG# 98

Doom And Gloom

The Rolling Stones just released their first new single in seven years. It's called "Doom and Gloom" and it got me thinking about all the media promoting doom and gloom.

Iran is going to have a nuclear bomb and destroy Israel and the Western world. Israel and the US won't let that happen so there will be a huge war that will lead to a world war because Russia, China, Syria and some radical terrorist groups support Iran.

Syria is going to drag Turkey into a war and the Arab nations will begin to fight each other which will disrupt the world's oil supply and lead to a world war. Africa is in melt down and terrorists are going to control the continent. To stop that from happening, the Western world will get into the fight which will lead to a big war.

Mexico is in a drug war and the drug lords will win and ship so many drugs to the world that everybody in America will become junkies. The United States and the European nations are going to create a financial disaster and the world economy will fail and everyone will be poor.

Roe vs Wade will be overturned and the states will make abortion illegal. Women who have an abortion will be arrested and charged with murder. Women will then rise up and overthrow the government. The rich will get richer and the middle class in America will be gone. Everyone will be either poor or rich (mostly poor) and the poor will rise up and overthrow the government.

Genetically engineered foods will give all of us health problems. Fast foods are going to kill us and make healthcare not affordable for most Americans. Everyone will become obese and die of heart disease and diabetes. If fast foods don't kill us, global warming will.

Unless you've been locked up in a small room in your basement, you've been bombarded with TV and the press pushing these dooms and gloom opinions down your throat. So called "experts" talk about this bad stuff like they know something. Radical TV hosts almost guarantee all this is going to happen. Even nationally trusted publications write about worse case scenarios.

The impact of all this doom and gloom has got to affect our mental well-being. The impact of all this doom and gloom is making many of us depressed. The impact of all this doom and gloom is making many of us see the future as negative instead of positive. The impact of all this doom and gloom makes us angry, frustrated and scared. The impact of all this doom and gloom could lead to a self-fulfilling prophecy (WAR).

What are the facts here? World War III is not going to happen. We're not going to blow up the world. We will not take away women's rights. The middle class will always be here because they're the largest voting block and will support the candidates who make middle class friendly policies. Drugs will always be around, but the majority will not let them affect their productivity.

Genetically engineered foods will not make us sick. Obesity will become unpopular and only affect the few, not the majority. The health industry will raise costs even if we shut down every fast food outlet. Pharmaceutical companies will eventually have a pill to fix all these problems because that's the way they make a shit load of money.

How do I know all this doom and gloom won't happen—just look at our history. We've lived through two world wars and came out stronger. We lived through the great depression and came out stronger. We lived through the drug days of the seventies and productivity increased. We gave women the right to vote.

Once 50 percent of the voters (women) were able to vote, women obtained more and more rights. In the long run, the people in power will not be able to take away all they gave to women. Women *will* eventually run this country.

Before all the current health rules came into place, most people's diets were terrible. They didn't live as long as us, but they did live and prosper. We've been eating genetically engineered foods for over twenty years and we haven't died. Global warming is really bad, but it's not going to affect *our* lives. I assume the generations after us will figure out a way to fix it.

Sooo, STOP worrying about all this gloom and doom. If possible, STOP reading, watching and listening to all this doom and gloom. Create a happy life for yourself and live it to the fullest. Believe the future is full of positive energy and everything will work out for the better. However, just in case the media is right:

Focus all your energy on today. Today is the day to find all the happiness you deserve. Don't let doom and gloom control your life.

BLOG# 99

Happy Holidays—Happy New Year

It's that time of year we all love and hate. We love getting time off from work. We love giving and getting presents. We love seeing friends and family. We love seeing other people happy. We love seeing houses and buildings decorated with holiday lights. We love the parties and the food. We love the thought that the New Year will be better than the current year. We just love the entire experience.

We hate the crowds pushing and shoving in the stores. We hate the holiday car drivers. We hate seeing people so poor they can't enjoy the holidays. We hate listening to people tell of their New Year resolutions they will never complete. We hate the negative energy people who are bah-humbug about the holidays. We hate the negative energy people who don't believe the New Year will be better than the last.

Happiness IS the forgotten ingredient in life. If there is ever a time to find happiness in your life, the holidays and the New Year is it. This is the time to enjoy all you've gotten. This is the time to enjoy all you've given. This is the time to enjoy everything that is about to happen. This is the time to feel good about the New Year.

This happiness can only happen if you decide to make it happen. That's right; you can decide to make the holidays and the New Year a happy time or a sad time. You can be positive about all the things you love about the holidays. You can also be positive about all the things you hate about the holidays.

It's up to you to ignore the pushing crowds, the bad drivers and the annoying negative energy people who don't like the holidays and believe the New Year will not be a happy one.

The one thing we shouldn't ignore is the people, who no fault of their own can't enjoy the holidays and the New Year the way we can. We can give something back to those people. We can remind ourselves how lucky we are and all we have. We can:

MAKE THE HOLIDAYS AND THE NEW YEAR THE BEST TIME OF OUR LIVES!

BLOG# 100

Happiness *IS* The Forgotten Ingredient In Life

If you've been reading my blogs you know my focus is happiness. Not their happiness—YOUR happiness. Why do I say it's the forgotten ingredient in life—because it is! Let's break down what I believe is important in your life. If I missed anything, please comment back to me.

Money

In my earlier blog I stated: "If you're happy, you'll have all the money you need. If you're unhappy, you'll never have enough money." Sooo, why are so many people willing to trade off their happiness to get more money? The answer is simple. Most people value money more than they value their happiness.

You might say: "I'd be happier if I had more money." Or, "don't give me that bullshit, everybody wants more money." Or, "I need more money to pay for all the things that make me happy." Or, "I don't value money more than happiness—I want more because money makes me happy." Or, "more money will make me feel secure."

None of the statements above are true. On the other hand, "money is NOT the root of all evil." People, who will compromise their moral compass, take advantage of other people, lie, cheat, steal and put their happiness in second position are the root of all evil.

Even the very poor can be happy if they appreciate friends, family and the beauty around them. Yes even in poor neighbors you can find beauty if you look at your environment with positive energy eyes instead of negative energy eyes. If the very poor can be happy without a lot of money, think about living your life with a positive attitude. More money is not the source of positive energy—YOU and your appreciation of life is what creates a positive attitude.

There is nothing wrong with having money. What's wrong is having the feeling you have to have more money to be happy. Therefore, stop making money the forgotten ingredient in life—make happiness the forgotten ingredient in life

Stuff

We are a society that accumulates lots of stuff. How many times have you cleaned out the garage or your closets of stuff? Do you say things like: "when did I buy that?" "I didn't even know I had that." "What was I thinking when I brought that." "I have to make more room because I'm going to buy more stuff." "These clothes are out of date, I need new ones." "I no longer fit into these pants, so I'm getting rid of them and get ones that fit."

Happiness IS the forgotten ingredient in life because we value "stuff" more than happiness. More stuff creates the need for more money. It becomes a vicious circle of wants verses needs. Could you be happy with what you have instead of getting caught up in a catch 22 of wants where happiness is taking a lower priority?

Too many people are caught up in this situation and have forgotten that happiness is their main goal, not more stuff. Their friends and family keep getting more stuff so they believe they should have more stuff. Before they know it, they have a lot of stuff, but it hasn't made them happier.

Somehow they believe if they just had even more stuff that would make them happier. It just doesn't work because happiness doesn't come from stuff. Happiness comes from appreciating the stuff you already have and feeling good that you can still be happy even though others have more. Don't make "stuff" the ingredient of life—make happiness the ingredient of life

Ego

One reason to have more stuff is to look good to others. Many say: "I don't buy expensive things for them; I buy it because it makes me feel good and that makes me happy." That statement is mucho, mucho bullshit. Too many people don't even realize what that statement means. First, it states you don't love yourself just the way you are. Second, it states the only way you can feel good about yourself is if you're wearing a Louis Vuitton bag, shirt and shoes.

The other part of that statement which is so not true is you do care what others think about how you look. Too many care so much about how they look, they're willing to make happiness a second thought. Buying expensive things means that you are accumulating more stuff and that makes you spend more money. If doing so doesn't really enhance your happiness, what good is it—absolutely nothing!

Happiness IS the forgotten ingredient in life because too many people value ego more than happiness. They believe they're not good enough unless they look good to others or to themselves. They don't feel beautiful inside so they believe they need a beautiful facade. Then they realize they need more stuff and more money to get the expensive stuff. This vicious negative circle gets them caught up on a focus where there is no room for happiness taking first position in their life.

Security

The need to feel secure has been drilled into all of us by our parents and their parents before them. There is nothing wrong with making security a priority. However, happiness winds up being the forgotten ingredient in life when people make security a higher priority. "If you're addicted to security, you will never have enough. If you prefer being secure, you will be able to balance your need for happiness with your need for security."

"I need more money to feel secure." I need more stuff to feel secure." "I need the outside world to see me as successful (ego) to feel secure." If you're making any one of those three statements you're addicted to security, you're insecure and you will trade your happiness to get more and more and more security.

Worrying about security is negative energy. It can make you become depressed. Depression is not a happy state. Worrying about the security problems you can't control (war, Iran, terrorist attack, earthquakes, stock market or a negative future), will never make you happy.

If you focus on the security things you can control (how much money you need so you can have food to eat, air to breath and shelter, how much insurance you need to protect your house, car, health or believing the future will be positive, not negative), you will be able to make happiness your first choice, not security.

"Happiness IS The Forgotten Ingredient In Life" because we make it so. If you really want to change your life, make a poster, put it into a beautiful frame and place it somewhere in your house or workplace where you'll have to see it every day. The poster should read:

"I Will Make Happiness The Most Important Focus Of My Life!"